NOTHING

BY DONNA BUISO

Published by Starry Night Publishing.Com

Rochester, New York

Copyright 2016 – Donna Buiso

Donna Buiso

"There's really no such thing as the 'voiceless'.
There are only the deliberately silenced, or the preferably unheard."

- Arundhati Roy

"There is no greater agony than bearing an untold story inside
you."

- Maya Angelou

Donna Buiso

DEDICATION

First and foremost to my children. Also to Celina and her son, and to all who have suffered as a result of the injustices of Probate Family Court rulings.

ACKNOWLEDGMENTS

Many thanks to my editor, Nicola, for her support and her patience, to Pam M, Carol A, Dr. Steve and Dr. O, to Cindy Barg and to my Jason's family, who emotionally keep me alive with their love, support and hugs.

FOREWORD

This book is a must-read for all, including Legislators, family and social agency workers, court and police officials, and all who recognize the vital importance of the family unit.

It should serve as a motivation for legislators to pass laws that demand greater accountability of our Probate Court system.

No single jurist should be able to decide the fate of a woman and her children, with no apparent and affordable right of appeal. No one individual should have such absolute god-like control over the lives of another person and her family.

This is a book that requires action. Action to change and rectify a system that allows the continued unconscionable abuse of mothers. These injustices must be corrected for the sake of all emotionally abused mothers, their emotionally abused children, and for the welfare of our society as a whole.

- David P. Hayes, Ph.D.

It is an absolute honor for me to acknowledge one woman's insurmountable, courageous journey to break the cycle of abuse with dignity and grace. Despite the horrific abuse Ms. Buiso endured, she broke the cycle. By sharing her own story, she gives a voice to all women.

Domestic violence is a pandemic, its prevalence sweeping, making it a commonplace and assumed behavior, grossly impacting women on all levels, emotionally, spiritually and physically. It does not discriminate. It stretches across national borders as well as socio-economic, cultural, racial and class notabilities. More importantly, domestic violence continues to exist without reproach and it is simply insupportable.

Ms. Busio's fight to end her abuse came at a price: isolation from her family and friends, exhaustion, betrayal, monetary depletion and pleas for help to lawyers and judges who continue to assert that domestic violence is an argument.

Abuse is about power and control. It is a learned behavior, not a sickness. It is a paramount public health issue that is terribly misunderstood and continues to be abandoned. Individuals who abuse are masters at believing their own deception. They abuse because they can.

Though physical abuse is horrific, emotional abuse is an insidious crime because there are no tangible wounds to affirm that the abuse ever took place. Emotional abuse magnifies with time and becomes intimately more threatening.

As. Ms. Buiso acclimated to the emotional abuse, the verbal strategies her husband inflicted upon her became an obscured reinforcement inside of her, making it more challenging for her to comprehend the extreme oppressiveness of the abuse. Until, one day, she had the fortitude to sever the toxic bond.

It is much easier to love in this lifetime than it is not to. The one single, ultimate element Ms. Busio's ex-husband can never take away from her is her truth. Her commitment to continue to educate women and to do so with great conviction, compassion and love will endure. *"I strongly believe that love is the answer and that it can mend even the deepest unseen wounds. Love can heal, love can console, love can strengthen, and yes, love can make change."* Somaly Mam

- Cindy Barg, M.Ed, LMHC, International Public Speaker, Psychotherapist and Author of the book, *But The Heavens Never Cried.*

Contents

PREFACE

Memories of my children and the events that led up to my losing them haunt me every day of my life. I wear their loss like a chronic disease. I never stop wondering about them or worrying about whether or not they are happy. Although I'm a grandmother, my days are focused on survival; both financial and emotional. I'm the bartender who works weekends and holidays and volunteers for the Christmas Eve shift. When one of my customers asks me about my family I have to choke to not cry. I smile in solidarity with the lonely regulars who frequent my bar on those special days when families like to gather. It helps me to keep busy at a job where I spend hours listening to the stories of others. They are my family now.

As much as I love my customers, bartending is hard work. I feel my age more and more each year. When I get home, I try to escape into the comfort of routine. I'm always greeted at the door of my basement apartment by my sweet feline friend of twelve years. Mona follows me around like a puppy. She waits patiently for me to kick off my shoes before she curls up on the sofa beside me.

On a Sunday evening in January, 2012, after working a particularly grueling shift, I set my purse down on the corner of my piano. My fingers ache to touch the keys. I can't remember how long it's been since I've played the music that used to soothe me. Tonight, my body is too tired to do anything but collapse on the couch. Tucking my legs under my hips, I pull a blanket over my lap to warm me from the chill of the night. Mona purrs lightly as I settle down to read the newspaper.

The front page of the local Times features a photograph of an adult hand holding a child's hand with the headline "A Mother's Fight." The words hit me like a punch to the stomach. I begin to shake as I read about a mother who is losing her battle to protect her young child from his father. The court, according to the reporter, continues to demand visitation for the father in spite of the mother's claims of sexual abuse.

The article goes on to explain how the judge continually questioned the mother's veracity in the face of overwhelming evidence against her ex-husband. Her story rocks me to my core as all the sick feelings I have regarding my own case surge through me once again. This is a story I've heard over and over, where abuse of a child is not prevented by a court system that is supposed to serve and protect.

I call the reporter at the newspaper and tell him that I want to reach out to the woman in his article to offer her my support. The reporter agrees to connect me with her and is interested in hearing about my story when I explain that it involves the same judge. In an email sent to the reporter after his interview, the judge had written, "Once a decision is made" he "rarely mulls it over again." The tragedy is that his decisions affect families for the rest of their lives.

Although it's been over a decade since my nightmare started, the stories about a court system that enables the abuse of children by granting custody, visitation or privileges to an abusive parent just keep surfacing. Many of these stories feature the mother as the perpetrator of a crime. The circumstances that drive a mother to 'kidnap' her own children and run away with them are rarely featured. They tend to focus on the arrest of the mother then wrap the whole ordeal up in a happy ending by featuring the return of the children to the father. I feel these stories in my gut. What about the truth behind the headline? Is this really a 'happy ending' for the children?

The destruction a judge's ruling can reap on a family can be irreparable. My own experience with Probate Court is just one example of how the court's corruption has been ruining lives for decades.

My voice was silenced when I was going through the worst ordeal any mother can imagine because the facts, letters and testimony in my case were not acknowledged by the court. My ex-husband is a master-manipulator and I was the proverbial frog in the pot of water that slowly came to a boil. I missed the signs until it was too late.

It only took a few years for my Prince Charming to destroy my life. First he took the money, then the business, the house, and finally the children. But this isn't a rant against my ex-husband. And this isn't just my story. It is every mother's story who ever fought to protect her children but got tangled up in the web of a broken court system.

I cannot die without being heard. This memoir contains copies of those documents the court refused to address when considering my case. I have redacted the names and locations on copies of legal documents and changed the names in my story to protect the innocent as well as the guilty. I am speaking my truth for myself, for my children, and for others who are being victimized. I refuse to 'go gentle into that good night.'

Donna Buiso

Chapter 1

NO GREATER LOVE

On the day my first child was born, in 1970, I woke up feeling happier than I'd ever felt before. Elizabeth was a tiny baby at 6 pound-4 ounces, and 18 inches long. She was beautiful. I remember looking out of the window of my hospital room in Western Massachusetts to see the sun shining over a perfect spring day. As I gazed down at my fragile, blue-eyed baby, I felt that life couldn't get any better. I was so overcome with love that I wondered if I'd died and gone to heaven.

My life revolved around my child from that moment on. I loved being a mother. Although I'd had dreams of going to art school I believed nothing could make me happier than being 'mommy' to Elizabeth. I couldn't take enough photographs and everything she did was an event. My parents, who were initially unhappy about the circumstances of my pregnancy, were soon doting on their first grandchild. It broke their hearts when, in 1972, I decided to move to Oceanside County, in Eastern Massachusetts, with Elizabeth's dad, Ron, to open a used clothing store with a couple of our friends.

Elizabeth was a happy child who seemed to have fun no matter where we were. She was the sweetest, prettiest little toddler who loved to play among the clothes' racks. I got the biggest kick out of her always asking for a 'lellow balana'.

Although we started off with a bang, our store was soon heading for demise. The combination of youth and too much partying was lethal to our business. It wasn't long before everyone bailed, including Ron, leaving me and Elizabeth to fend for ourselves. In spite of everything, I felt blessed because I had Elizabeth. We were always together.

After Ron left, I didn't always have a working car so Elizabeth and I often hitched a ride to the beach. In 1972 everyone was hitching a ride somewhere. A real hippie child, my daughter wore a little jean jacket and a skull cap and would stick her thumb out, just like I did, until we got a ride. I loved the ocean and so did Elizabeth. We had a lot of fun playing tag.

While I sunbathed, she'd shave my legs with a seashell, or water the sand with her little pail. We even took a ride in a small plane one afternoon, gasping in awe as we looked down to see our neighborhood surrounded by ocean. Although we rarely left the area we did take some trips to New Hampshire, with my Cousin Gina's family, where we'd have a great time cross-country skiing.

We ended up moving a lot but I made sure that no matter how often we moved, we stayed in the same town so that Elizabeth wouldn't have to change schools. I taught her to play piano. She was a natural and full of confidence, mastering "New York, New York" enough to play it in a talent show at eleven. She took dance lessons from age seven and loved it enough to eventually become a Performing Arts Major at Emerson College, and later to teach choreography at local theater. I reveled in all her high school musicals, college performances, and watching her sing and dance in local theaters. I'll always remember how proud and happy I was to watch her performance as one of the orphans in her high school production of Annie and how touched I felt when she ran off the stage at the end of the show to hug me. We shared our love of all things artistic and I think she intuitively knew that I lived vicariously through her.

Being a single mom wasn't easy but the two of us got by. Trying to find reliable people to babysit while I worked was always a challenge. At one point, when Elizabeth was about nine years old, I was desperately in need of a babysitter. One of my neighbors recommended a teenage girl who lived in the neighborhood.

Paula was a sixteen-year-old bubbly, red-haired ball of grins and energy. It was hard to believe that she had spent her life in foster homes. Elizabeth loved her and so did I. A young Beatles fan, she and I spent a lot of time raving about our favorite songs. I always felt peaceful going to work knowing that Paula was with Elizabeth. One night, however, I was shocked when Paula came over to babysit wearing a brace around her neck.

"Paula, what happened?" I cried, rushing toward her.

"Ida came home drunk and threw me against the wall. I sprained my neck."

"And you're still living there?"

"DSS has nowhere else to place me. They are looking, but if they don't find someone else to foster me then I'll have to go into a group home in Springfield until I'm eighteen. I don't want to go. I'll run away first."

I hugged her and asked her if this had ever happened before. She told me that her foster mom was always drunk. Paula was the cook, maid and babysitter for Ida's young sons. Ida never spent a dime on Paula, even though DSS sent extra checks a few times a year for essentials, like clothing and toiletries.

I went to work but was barely able to think about anything except what Paula had told me. I came home that night, weighed the pro's and con's, then decided that there was no way I could turn my back on her situation. Paula was already part of our little family. The only difference would be that she'd be living with us. I was only in my twenties and wasn't sure I was capable of mothering a teen, but I knew anything would be better than what she was dealing with in her foster home.

Paula came by nearly every day, even if she wasn't babysitting, so it wasn't long before I had the opportunity to ask her if she wanted me to be her foster mother. I wasn't sure I'd be accepted and I let her know that. She was ecstatic at my suggestion. To my surprise, DSS didn't blink an eye about giving me custody of her under the provision that I would attend the classes that DSS held for foster parents to aid them in their endeavor. I happily complied and felt relief that I would have support in this major decision.

On the day that Paula was to come and live with us, Elizabeth and I got the house ready for her and cooked her favorite meal for dinner. After all the excitement that had built up between the three of us it was a letdown to see Paula quietly go upstairs to the bedroom she was to share with Elizabeth. She didn't even want to eat the dinner we had so lovingly prepared. The next day, she didn't come down from her room but continued to sleep. I became so concerned that I called her social worker who informed me that this was very common with foster kids. For better or worse, it was another transition and this was her way of escaping. The social worker assured me that it would pass and it did. Paula was soon back to her old self, allowing me to love and spoil her, just like I did Elizabeth. Within the year I found a three bedroom house so that we could all have our own room.

Eastern Massachusetts, 1981

I was working in the lounge of a new gym when I met Dave. The General Manager of the club, he had a local reputation for being a super athlete and was loved nationally by racquetball enthusiasts. All the employees seemed to respect him, as did the clients who relied on him for racquetball lessons. It was easy to be drawn to his handsome face and well-toned athlete's body, but I was also drawn to his caring and charismatic personality. I loved my job and was very happy in my new home with my girls. For the first time in years, I felt secure.

Paula was a teenager with a busy social life so I often took Elizabeth to work with me. She would sit in the lounge and do her homework or play ping pong in the game room. One night Jay, my boyfriend at the time, came to the gym with his daughter who was the same age as Elizabeth. The girls were having so much fun together that Jay asked if Elizabeth could go home with them and spend the night. I agreed.

The next morning, I called Jay's house to tell Elizabeth that I was going to take both girls to the beach. As I was gathering towels and beach accessories the phone rang. It was Elizabeth screaming into the phone that Jay's dog, Bing, had attacked her and that she was "full of holes."

I felt like I was moving in slow motion as I drove to Jay's house. Even though we only lived a few miles away, that was the longest ride of my life. The ambulance was already there when I arrived. I remember running into the house to find Elizabeth lying on the couch covered in blood and dog hair. She calmly told me that the paramedics had talked about her getting plastic legs. She was in shock and I was too. I couldn't think about what had just happened or what was going to happen. My mind wouldn't allow it. I could only think about being with Elizabeth, one moment at a time.

The nearest hospital was on strike but the Emergency Room was open. I managed to keep myself together in my daughter's presence but when she was out of sight I fell apart. The ER doctor told me how lucky we were that Bing didn't puncture a main artery, bite off a finger or tear her face.

Elizabeth was transferred to another local hospital for surgery and I spent what seemed like hours pacing the waiting room floor and bumping into walls. A nurse snapped me back to reality when she tapped me on the shoulder and handed me a pair of paper hospital slippers. I had run out of the house barefoot.

Over the next week Elizabeth underwent several surgeries and I slept on a cot in her room for the first few nights of recovery. She was so brave. Her stuffed animal, Belle, wore a hospital bracelet just like hers.

The hospital was overflowing due to the strike at Oceanside County Hospital and every bed was needed. Elizabeth was released before she could walk. My father had carried her on his back to the car as he enthused about a surprise he had waiting for her at home. He'd rigged up cable so that she could watch television in her room. None of her friends had a TV in their bedroom so it was a big treat.

Physically, Elizabeth healed quickly but she had to learn to walk again. Emotionally, she was plagued with nightmares and filled with a fear of all dogs. All I could concentrate on during the first months after the accident was Elizabeth's physical and emotional recovery. She had multiple appointments with a specialist a half hour drive in one direction and counseling sessions a half hour's drive in the opposite direction. It was hard for me to keep track of Paula who spent a lot of time hanging out with her friends. She had also fallen in love with her boyfriend Bob. He was a couple of years older than her and I suspected that he was a controlling influence when he made it clear that he didn't want to spend much time at our house.

The emotional strain of Elizabeth's accident was hard to hide at work. Dave was continually asking me about my daughter and offering me compassion and advice. About six months after Elizabeth's accident, Dave promoted me to bar manager which gave me closer contact with him on a daily basis. The more I got to know him the more attractive he became to me. I knew he was involved with someone but his girlfriend was rarely around and I was single again. Although I didn't blame him, Jay suffered massive guilt about his dog attacking Elizabeth and he couldn't seem to bear to be around us. This made Dave's attention all the more enticing.

I was feeling particularly overwhelmed one afternoon about everything that had happened to Elizabeth, when Dave walked over to the bar and stared at me with his deep brown eyes. "How would you like to take a ride on my motor cycle?" he asked. Of course I said yes and will never forget how quickly my body let go of the tension I'd been clinging to as we sped along winding, ocean-side streets.

We appeared to have a lot in common and we both came from big extended Italian families. When I made it clear that family is very important to me Dave told me about his love and respect for his aunts and uncles. This resonated with me because I grew up so close to my own aunts, uncles and cousins. He seemed to understand that Elizabeth was my world. He treated her with kindness and often expressed how he couldn't wait to become a father. "I don't understand how men can cheat on their wives and hurt their children," he'd say. I looked at him and I saw a man with values. I focused on his charm, which he reinforced at every opportunity.

I was also greatly impressed by Dave's intelligence. Whenever we were alone together he'd tell me all about his various business ideas and his plans to implement them. I couldn't pretend to understand everything he was saying but he obviously had some serious goals and I admired him for that. I soon came to believe that he was my Prince Charming and I let myself fall in love. Elizabeth wasn't happy when Dave and I became a couple but I hoped that she would come to love him in time.

After she started back to school in the fall Elizabeth would run home from the bus stop terrorized whenever she saw a dog. I realized that the only way for her to conquer this fear was to get a loving dog for herself.

We selected Millie from the Animal Rescue League after it was clear that we all connected. I believe Millie was sent by God, not only for Elizabeth, but for me too. She was the sweetest and gentlest of God's creatures and she did heal my daughter. The little girl who had become so terrified of dogs would hold an umbrella over Millie so that she could pee without getting wet. We took Millie to the beach and she loved it. I remember Elizabeth pretending to drown one day and crying "Help Millie!" The dog, who never wanted to get her paws wet, dove in without hesitation to help her.

Through all of the drama with Elizabeth's accident, I saw less and less of Paula as she became more involved with Bob. She eventually moved in with him. Her social worker and I got together often and his concern was the same as mine; that in her need to be loved she would become pregnant. Paula gave birth to a son shortly after her eighteenth birthday.

I had often talked to Paula about me adopting her after she turned eighteen, when it would be an easier process than while she was still a minor. It soon became clear that Bob was controlling and jealous of Paula's ties to me. After her eighteenth birthday I sent Paula the necessary paperwork for adoption, only to have it intercepted by Bob who would have none of it. The adoption would have to wait another twenty years.

Chapter 2

RED FLAGS

Throughout our early dating, Dave would often bring up Elizabeth's accident and ask me what I was doing about litigation. Eventually I did talk to a lawyer. I had medical bills to pay and Elizabeth deserved something for the emotional and physical scars that she bears to this day. Dave would periodically inquire, "Do you trust this lawyer? Are you sure he's doing right by you?" I thought he was being supportive. After being together for a several months, however, red flags began to pop up that should have tainted my rose-colored glasses.

One of the first red flags appeared during a dinner out with three other couples. Dave was talking about his grandiose business plans and when I tried to interject, he said, "Can't listen to her. No college degree there!" Dave and I had the same amount of schooling. He'd dropped out before graduating in his fourth year of college. I already had an Associate's Degree and was a year away from completing my Bachelor's degree. I'd gone through college being a single parent and working four nights a week but still managed to stay on the Dean's list every semester, so why was he insulting my intelligence? I'd confronted him about it at home but he'd lovingly put his arms around me and said that he'd meant no harm by it and was just trying to be funny. "Don't be so sensitive" he'd chided as he flashed me his charming smile.

Another red flag appeared when Dave started making derogatory remarks about my cooking to friends. He knew that I took great pains to cook for my family, almost always buying fresh supplies and making everything from scratch. I would question him about his negative comments but once again he would flash me his beguiling smile and caution me not to overreact.

Dave's subtle and then not-so-subtle put-downs bothered me at first, but he always convinced me that I was being overly sensitive to what he felt was humor. We both had dogs when we got together but he'd argue that his dog was much smarter than my poor "stupid Millie." I'd wanted so much to believe that he was the perfect man that I began to believe I did overreact to his hostile humor and that I was ultrasensitive.

His criticisms extended to my family when he started to complain about how classless my parents were. "It's not that I don't like them, but when my parents host their annual cookout we'd rather your parents don't come," he said as he put his arm around my shoulder and gave me a light kiss on the head. "You don't have to hurt their feelings. Just make an excuse. You understand don't you, hon?"

Dave started sleeping over every night until he essentially moved in with me and Elizabeth. As much as he said he understood how hard I struggled as a single mom, he never offered to contribute anything to the household. When we celebrated our first Christmas as a live-in couple he told me that a water bed he'd won at a racquetball tournament was my Christmas gift. I felt deep disappointment but never expressed it to him for fear of appearing ungrateful. Wasn't the waterbed something he would be sleeping in as well? I would have been thrilled with a candle – something personal that showed he'd thought about me. I chalked it up to it being "a guy thing" and tried not to make too much of it.

One night, around ten o'clock, our neighbors were making a lot of noise in their driveway, which was right next to our bedroom window. The noise wasn't unusual, but when I heard a heated exchange outside the window I realized that it was between them and Dave. To my horror I watched as Dave retrieved a shot gun that he kept hidden in the bedroom closet. He then pointed it out the window at the neighbors.

"Where did that gun come from?" I yelled.

"Don't worry. It's not loaded. I just want to scare them."

Scare them he did. They called the police. A few minutes later, Dave and the police held a civil conversation about the rifle and no charges were filed. The gun was put back in its hiding place and that was the end of it. I didn't want a gun in the house but Dave refused to get rid of it. He promised me that he didn't have ammunition for the gun. Of course I believed him.

No matter what happened, I always accepted Dave's word in the end; even the night he almost strangled me.

We had fallen asleep after a quiet evening of watching TV together. I woke up in the dead of night trying to scream and opened my eyes to see Dave sitting on me with his hands around my throat. He was looking right at me. As our eyes met he started laughing hysterically as he climbed off me.

"My God, Dave! What the hell are you doing?" I choked as I sat up in the bed.

"I must have been dreaming," he laughed, as though it was the funniest thing he'd ever done.

I couldn't stop shaking.

"Come on now! You know I'd never hurt you. I was just dreaming! It's funny." He'd pulled me down and cuddled me, once again convincing me that it really was no big deal.

In spite of all this I was madly in love with him. I ignored the red flags and focused on his good qualities and how loving he could be. We were engaged within the year.

September, 1984

The more involved I became with Dave, the less communication I had with Paula. I was anxious to tell her about my engagement but my ties to her were already thin because of Bob's control of her. Dave and I both agreed on a modest wedding with about a hundred guests. There was no question that Elizabeth would be my Maid of Honor and my cousin Gina was adamant about being my Matron of Honor. "We've been like sisters all our lives," she'd pleaded. "Of course I should be standing up for you!" Dave was unhappy about Gina being involved and he didn't miss an opportunity to tell me how much he disliked her.

"She doesn't care about you, D. She just mooches off of us; always coming around at dinner time. Look at the cheap souvenirs she brought us back from her vacation. Like that makes up for all the free meals! She also thinks she should get a break on a gym membership. I don't think so!"

Dave wanted his sister to be a bridesmaid and that was fine with me. Even though Paula and I rarely talked she was still an important part of my life and I wanted to include her in the wedding party. After his reaction to Gina, I knew it wouldn't be a good idea to argue with him about Paula, although I did make an attempt. I waited until we were alone and Dave was in a good mood before I announced that I needed to talk about some of the wedding plans.

"You know how I feel about Paula. She's like a daughter to me. I want to include her in my wedding. It just won't feel right without her."

He'd pondered a minute as he looked into the distance before responding. "Okay, D. How about this? I think it would be an honor for Paula to greet our guests at the reception. Only a family member would be trusted to do that. She'll feel so special."

His tone made it clear that there was no room for discussion so I reluctantly agreed, ignoring the gnawing in my gut that I felt about Paula's meager participation in this huge event in my life. I was trained to believe that Dave always knew better. After all, he made all the important decisions regarding our wedding reception, although he did let me pick the location for the actual wedding. I sought out a nondenominational church for our ceremony. After I attended services for a few Sundays to get a feel for it, I fell in love with the church's message. I asked the Minister to preside over our marriage and he agreed.

On the day of our wedding, Paula stood at the door of the reception with her husband. I hugged her and we had a brief conversation but Bob stood close by as though he were monitoring what we said to each other. I had the sense that all was not well between them and that Paula was not comfortable.

Despite my concerns over Paula's happiness, my wedding day was one of the happiest days of my life. Dave's family, whom I'd embraced as my own, all traveled to celebrate with us. We had a special table at the reception for our dearest friends and members of our gym. I made a speech and tearfully expressed how happy I was to have everyone I loved in the same room.

I noticed that Paula disappeared shortly after the reception started. I did talk to her a few days later and found out that Bob had insisted on them leaving early. Although my wedding and reception was a wonderful day for me it was tainted by an uneasy feeling that I'd let Paula down.

I decided to join the church we were married in. As a Music Major, I was drawn to the small choir and quickly became a member of that as well. I loved singing and had taken voice lessons and sung for many years with the Oceanside County Community College Chorus. I hadn't realized how much I missed it. Music had always been a huge part of my life and being part of a small choir was so exciting for me. Dave started to come to church with me as well. We had something else to share and everything felt so right; at least almost everything.

As happy as I was, I felt like I was losing my identity. Dave had started calling me DW (Dave's Wife). I never liked it, especially when he introduced me to others that way. I struggled to keep a hold of the things that were so important to me. Once Dave realized that I still had my own checking account he confronted me. "You're a married woman now. Why do you insist on having your own checking account? Don't you trust me?" I was convinced that I was being selfish so I dissolved my account and opened a joint checking account with Dave.

My connection to Paula was now hanging by a thread. I missed her, but I assumed that she was happy and that her life was as crazy busy as mine was. We didn't live close by and we lost touch for months but we'd always reconnect at some point. She contacted me about the big events in her life, like the birth of her two children and I remember visiting her in the hospital when she had her second child.

I was allowed in shortly after the birth because I was the 'grandmother'. It got me several skeptical looks as I was barely into my thirties. I also occasionally visited Paula and her children in their home where most of our conversations were centered on the children.

Summer, 1985

It wasn't long before I became pregnant with my son Evan. Neither Elizabeth nor I had anticipated that I'd ever have more children. Although I had tried for nine months, it was a surprise when I found out that I was pregnant. It didn't seem as though it was going to happen so when it did there was a lot of excitement. Dave couldn't wait to call his parents and hear his mother scream for joy into the phone.

I not only remember the day I told Elizabeth that I was pregnant, I also remember the day I told her that she was going to have a little brother. I had an ultra-sound when I was four months pregnant and saw a baby boy with his thumb in his mouth. Elizabeth and I had hugged and cried for joy.

I had the easiest pregnancy. The only thing reminding me that I was pregnant was my growing belly. Elizabeth and I attended a duet piano concert when I was in my ninth month and Evan was a constant metronome. Elizabeth was astounded when I put her hand on my belly and we both marveled at how he kicked quickly in response to the fast music then slowly to the slower pieces. It would be our earliest indication of his musical abilities.

March, 1986

A trial date for Elizabeth's accident was scheduled for two weeks before Evan was born. It had been three years since the accident. Elizabeth was awarded a one hundred thousand dollar settlement for hospital bills and for her pain and suffering. Whatever was left after the bills were paid was to go into a trust fund for Elizabeth. However, all she cared about was my promise to take her clothes shopping and have a special dinner with her when the money came through. We made plans to go celebrate later in the week before the baby arrived.

28

The night after the trial, Dave announced that he had something to discuss with me and Elizabeth. He knew about the plans for Elizabeth's money, but he said he'd got a better plan.

After we were married I had given up my rental home and moved into Dave's house. It was in a questionable part of town and Elizabeth hated living there. Dave proposed that we put his house in my name on behalf of Elizabeth and then rent it out. Then we would use Elizabeth's settlement money to buy a house in a better neighborhood. At first, I balked at his suggestion, but as he went on with his argument about how cramped we would be with the new baby coming and how Elizabeth wanted to get out of the area, I agreed to hear him out.

"This house would be Elizabeth's equity," Dave calmly explained. "We could pay for her to go college to make up for any accumulated interest she would get."

The more he talked, the more Elizabeth got excited and they both hounded me about how much sense it made. Elizabeth looked at me with pleading eyes. I looked at her and then at Dave. I loved Dave and I wanted to trust him. After all, I was about to have his baby.

A few days later, I turned the settlement check over to Dave. He told me he'd open a secure, high interest account and agreed to give me a few hundred dollars off the top so that Elizabeth and I could splurge a little, as planned. I asked him for the money, a couple of days later, but he refused to give it me. "It would be stupid for you to buy clothes when you're about to have a baby, and Elizabeth doesn't really need anything. Maybe another time."

Elizabeth looked at me pleadingly and I reiterated to Dave that this was a promise I had made to my daughter and wanted to keep. He begrudgingly gave me a little money to take her to the mall to buy her a few items of clothing. It was nothing like the big 'splurge' that we had looked forward to but I saw it as a compromise. Once again, I gave Dave the benefit of the doubt by telling myself that he was just trying to be frugal and protective of Elizabeth's money.

On the Thursday before Evan was born Dave and I got into a horrible fight. I don't remember the details of the argument but I do remember the rage he expressed by screaming at me and getting in my face. Elizabeth was so upset she'd tried to intervene. "Dave, please stop! She's pregnant. You can't do this to her!"

I'd sat sobbing in the rocking chair all night. I could barely drag my swollen belly around the next day because I was so tired. The following night, I had mild cramps that kept me awake. By morning I was in full labor.

Although my pregnancy was easy and I had continued to play racquetball and worked right up until the day before I went into labor, my labor was very difficult. I was exhausted from the fight, and as I'd decided on an all-natural birth, I just didn't have the strength I needed going into it. Elizabeth stayed by my side the whole time. She held my hand for hours, brought me ice chips and stroked my brow. Dave walked around socializing with the doctors, nurses and anyone who would chat with him, when he wasn't engrossed in the March Madness basketball games on the hospital room TV.

Just before Evan was born, the doctor declared that only one person could be in the room with me during the actual birth. He asked Elizabeth to leave. I tried to speak to appeal to the doctor to let her stay but he ignored me. Elizabeth held my hand until she had to let it go, then she tearfully left the room. The only memory I have of Dave in the delivery room was during the most painful part of my labor, when I felt sure I was going to pass out. I overheard him telling a joke to the doctor and attending nurses. I yelled at him to shut up but he just laughed.

I vividly remember that when I saw Evan for the first time, all the pain was forgotten. He was born with a 'cone-head' but it didn't prevent me from thinking he was perfect. I was engulfed by instant love. The doctor allowed Elizabeth back into the room and I saw the love that I was experiencing in her face as she held her baby brother. I watched Dave as he held his son for the first time and I recognized the man I'd fallen in love with.

The next morning, Dave came to visit me in the hospital and brought a bunch of celebratory balloons. I thanked him as I kissed him.

"Thank your daughter," he smirked. "She made me do it."

Evan had been born on a Saturday evening. I was back to work at our gym on Monday morning with my newborn in tow. Our life immediately seemed to go back to normal, except that we had a new family member. Dave spent most of his time at the gym but I was too busy to be lonely. Elizabeth doted on her brother, and although I never would impose on her, she seemed unable to get enough of him and insisted on helping me with him.

In June, Dave bought our marital home in the village of Seaville with Elizabeth's settlement money. He arrived home and casually announced, "I want to show you the house we're getting." I wondered why Elizabeth and I weren't included in the house hunt but when I saw the home I didn't care. It was everything I'd ever dreamed of.

Of course, Dave decided the layout of the home. My only concern was moving my cherished piano and placing it in a place where I could comfortably play. I found the ideal place for it against the dining room wall. Although I didn't get to play nearly as much as I wanted, it was comforting to be able to sit before the keys, even for a few minutes, and play my heart out.

Dave claimed a big room in the back of the house for his office where he often spent hours at his desk "doing paperwork." I was talking to him in the office one evening when I caught a glimpse of the deed to our new house sitting on the desk. "Where is my name?" I asked.

He shrugged. "D, everything is held fifty-fifty in a marriage in Massachusetts. This is your house as much as it is mine. Having your name on the deed is just a formality."

I reached for the deed. "But shouldn't my name be on it too?"

He grabbed it from my hand. "If you don't believe me, why don't you ask my cousin Gil about it next time you see him? I'm sure he'd be happy to discuss it with you."

Gil was an attorney. We ran into him a few days later at a family gathering. As soon as Dave saw him at the grille, where he was barbequing steaks, he yelled, "Hey Gil, isn't it true that all marital assets are owned fifty-fifty between a husband and wife in this state?"

"Definitely," Gil nodded as he returned to his grilling.

That was enough for me. In my naiveté, I had no idea what not having my name on the deed could really lead to. I let it go and concentrated on my new baby.

Dave was rarely home and Elizabeth was often at school or out with friends so Evan and I spent most of our time together. When he was very tiny I would bring him to work with me and prop him on my desk in his infant seat. As he became a toddler I put him in the nursery at our gym where I could keep a close eye on him. He was an amazing toddler. As soon as he could pull himself up, at around six months old, he'd dance to our singing Chitty Chitty Bang Bang while wiggling his butt all over the place. That's also when I started reading to him. At seven months old Evan would pick up a book, then pull himself up onto my knees and hand it to me to read to him. We'd spend hours outside pulling his little red wagon, which he would fill with rocks, as we walked.

Evan could count to three by his first birthday. . Elizabeth was studying Spanish in school and I had taken Spanish in high school, so we often spoke Spanish to each other in front of Evan. He could count to twenty in Spanish by his second birthday. I remember going through the check-out at the supermarket and him counting the items in Spanish as they went by him. I thought the sales girl was going to faint.

Although Evan was just a toddler, Dave began to bully him into doing things that scared him. He followed our son around, once he started learning to walk, urging him to go faster. Dave would then laugh like hell when Evan fell over. Dave also liked to jump around corners to scare him, again, laughing as Evan cried. My motherly concerns over this behavior were always minimized by Dave. "Stop being a smothering mother. You'll make a mama's boy out of him. Let us have some fun."

Dave came home one evening and announced that the owners of the gym had decided not to renew the liquor license for the lounge that I managed. He said he wanted to buy the lounge. "We can take out a mortgage on this house," he enthused. "It will be worth it. Members love going up to the bar after a work-out." I honestly thought it was a great idea.

After we bought the lounge it wasn't long before we bought the whole gym by taking another mortgage on our marital home. I was really happy to be able to do this because I loved the business so much. Dave and I, Elizabeth and even Evan practically lived at the gym. It was our home away from home. All the members knew us and they were happy with the new ownership arrangement. One of our members was a reporter for the local newspaper. Feeling that I didn't get enough recognition, he interviewed me for an article entitled "The Woman Behind The Man" in which I raved about my love of the business and the people I had come to know as my gym family.

Dave and I were "Mom" and "Pop" at the gym. We became close friends with many of the members, going out to dinner and nightclubs together. We celebrated birthdays and holidays with many of them. We also hosted racquetball tournaments and big Christmas parties where Dave and I would greet the members as they came in the door.

The moment I dared to believe that I had it all is when then things began to change.

On the surface, I played the game, but I was becoming increasing uncomfortable with Dave's behavior, especially in relation to his treatment of Elizabeth. What I didn't notice him doing to me, I did notice him do to her. He started criticizing Elizabeth consistently and screamed at her whenever he was angry. When she announced that she wanted to explore a relationship with her biological father Dave freaked out and chased her down the street, yelling at her like a lunatic. He'd later forced her into a chair and demanded (at age 15) that she choose which 'father' she wanted to walk her down the aisle when she got married. She'd cried and looked stunned, unable to answer him as he continued to scream at her. I'd stood in disbelief as he insisted on answers that she was unable to give. I remember him darting a look in my direction, daring me to intervene. After he finally stormed off, I'd tried to comfort Elizabeth and tell her that it was only because he loved her so much that he got so upset. "I'm so sorry, Elizabeth, but Dave feels that HE is your father and we are a family now. He doesn't want anything to disrupt that." I was trying to convince myself as much as her.

Elizabeth's father, Ron, had never paid child support and I had never pursued it. He had rarely been around and was not a big part of our lives. I was content just to have Elizabeth and always felt sad for what Ron was missing. Once Dave came into the picture, he insisted that I go after Ron for child support. His arguments made sense to me because child support would improve the quality of Elizabeth's life. I went along with Dave and felt that I was doing the right thing. The courts did approve my petition and Dave was quick to claim victory. "If it wasn't for me, she wouldn't be getting anything from her father because you never would have pursued it on your own."

Ron wanted to know what became of Elizabeth's settlement money. Dave responded by hiring an attorney for me to go after Ron for back child support. I quickly blocked out of my mind the shameful memory of going along with Dave and the lawyer and having Elizabeth testify against her biological father, just as she was trying to get to know him and form a meaningful relationship with him.

Although Dave claimed to have no prejudices, he discouraged blacks and gays from joining our gym. "It's just business D. Get off my back," he'd retort whenever I complained. I was mortified but couldn't change his mind. A lot of Elizabeth's friends liked to hang out at our house because we had a finished basement. Once she started dating, the boys came over too. On one occasion, Elizabeth came home with a young black man. Dave was cordial enough to the boy while he was in our home, but after he left, Dave lost it. "How can you bring home a black kid without warning me first? What's the matter with you?" he'd screamed at her. "Do you know how upsetting this will be to my parents?" Elizabeth had no idea what she'd done wrong. She was developing into a beautiful young woman and this boy was only one of many crushes she'd had at fifteen.

Dave noticed her developing too. I became increasingly disturbed when he would pull Elizabeth onto his lap, tickle her on the bed, and stroke her back while she was sitting watching TV. More than one person took me aside and questioned his inappropriate behavior.

I was careful not to accuse Dave of anything but once we were alone, in the privacy of our bedroom, I gently suggested that his physicality with Elizabeth made me uncomfortable. I added that a few people had commented on it. He started screaming.

"What are you accusing me of, D....? How evil minded are you? You would actually think I'm capable of whatever your dirty little mind is conjuring up? Just because your family is crazy, and they all have dirty minds, you don't have to go along with them," he'd raged. "I've tried to be a good father to that girl and here I am, simply trying to show her affection, and this is how I'm treated?"

I felt ashamed for bringing it up, convinced that Dave would never do anything unseemly. What was wrong with me? Besides, I was pregnant again. This man was to be the father of two of my children. What was I thinking?

January, 1988

Elizabeth and Evan were my 'laid-back' children. My third child, Amy Rose, was anything but laid-back. Even before she was born she was constantly kicking to get out so it was no surprise when she was born a week early.

I'd had another easy pregnancy and this time my labor wasn't as intense because I'd decided on an epidural. Once again, Dave enjoyed himself chatting to the doctor about golf over my painfully contracting belly.

Amy was beautiful from the minute she was born. She had reddish peach fuzz for hair and a Burt Lancaster dimple in the middle of her chin. Even the doctor remarked on what a beautiful baby she was. As she was handed to me I could feel my heart swelling with love. I noticed that she had the same big blue eyes as my Elizabeth.

I remember waking up at three o'clock the morning after giving birth. I felt something was wrong with Amy and called the nurses' station. "Please bring me my baby. She's crying for me."

"Now dear, how would you know that? You cannot hear the nursery from here," the nurse had tried to placate me.

"She's crying. I just know it. Please bring her to me!"

The nurse gave in and came back with my wailing daughter. She placed her in my arms where Amy immediately quieted down. The nurse smiled. "There's no stronger bond than a mother and her baby."

I brought Amy home to a chaotic house. With a brother only 21 months older than her and a teenage sister who was getting ready to graduate high school, my days were a blur of activity. I didn't have much time to consider what was going on in my life beyond my children.

May, 1988

Graduation was a big deal for Elizabeth, but what she was really excited about was her prom. It was a huge event for me as well. We had such fun looking for her prom dress. She found one she loved that made her look like a beautiful southern belle. Her date and some of her friends all came to the house before leaving for the prom in their limo. Dave and I took pictures of them and some of me with Elizabeth. I was so happy to be involved.

Elizabeth was planning to attend college in the fall. With two babies to keep me busy, I was happy to let Dave go over the logistics of college paperwork with her. I fully expected that Dave and I would pay for all her college expenses and did not realize that he had been instructing Elizabeth to take out student loans.

I drove Elizabeth to Boston and checked out her dorm. It seemed that I had barely dropped her off before she was calling me to chat about all the details of her roommate, the 'haunting' of the dorm, the bad food in the cafeteria and all the exciting details of her student life. I was also relieved that she would have a break from Dave. The summer before she left for college she had moved in with a friend of mine to get away from him. It broke my heart, but I knew I had to get used to her absence.

As much as I missed Elizabeth, I didn't have time to mope. My days were all about Evan and Amy. In the mornings, we curled up on the couch together to watch Sesame Street and Mr. Rogers. In the afternoons we had fun exploring different playgrounds in the area.

Amy was fearless, always trying to climb higher and faster than she should. I felt for sure that she would be the one to give me my first gray hair. Evan was the cautious child. At home we used to play music; John Souza was one of our favorites and we'd march around the house blaring his music. Rafi was another favorite, especially "Baby Beluga." I cherished every moment of being with my children.

Most of the time, Evan and Amy got along great, but sometimes Evan would annoy Amy or tease her when she was in her walker. Amy didn't cry. She'd push herself over to him and give him a pinch which would make him scream at the top of his lungs. She was my feisty little girl who melted my heart every time she sang "Skinamarinky-dinky-doo, I love you…" always putting her hands over her heart and then opening them wide on the "I love you" part. I noticed that Dave wasn't as hard with Amy as he was with Evan. I summed it up as Amy being "Daddy's little girl."

Dave spent a lot of time on our boat and loved to take friends out on it. One weekend, our friends, Paul and Rita, were visiting from Western Mass and Dave was excited to take them on the boat. Paul was up for it but Rita decided she wanted to stay behind with me and the kids. I wasn't comfortable taking them aboard together because it was hard enough to watch Evan with an infant in my arms on land.

After we drove down to the dock where the boat was moored, Paul, Rita and I stood and chatted while Dave got ready to launch. Dave was ready to roll but at the last minute he yelled at me to "toss" Evan up to him. "Let him hang out with the men."

As I stood there trying to come up with excuses, Dave jumped off the boat, scooped Evan up then jumped aboard. I turned to Rita with pleading eyes. "Please go with them!!"

She patted my hand. "I'll go and I'll hold him tight," she assured me, flashing me a "don't worry" look as she swung herself over the rail of the boat.

As I watched them sail down the channel I realized what had just transpired; I was not comfortable leaving my children's safety in the hands of their own father.

It took me a while, but when I finally realized what was happening to my children I emerged out of my coma and started to speak up. This only infuriated Dave even more and prompted him to step up his verbal and emotional abuse. He constantly accused me of being evil-minded, an incompetent mother and an over-reactor. I was just beginning to get glimmers of insight as to what was really going on, but I still believed that a lot of the problem was with me. I'd allowed Dave to railroad me and gone along for the ride as he totally took over our lives. With no voice, there was no room for compromise. I lost my soul and feel humiliated to think that I was manipulated into going along with his schemes.

It wasn't just the yelling and taunting that became worse. Our sex life began to feel like rape. Dave would come home late at night and force sex on me. There was no conversation and no cuddling. He satisfied himself while I cried. He either didn't notice or he didn't care. This was when I first suspected that he might be cheating, or at least thinking about it. He was often out late and seemed to come home "preheated."

Dave was home less and less, which was a relief to me, and although I was increasingly unhappy, I was totally wrapped up in my children. Mothering them was my escape. I had a home I absolutely loved, a business I was proud of and beautiful children whom I adored. I took Evan and Amy with me to play in the gym's nursery while I worked. I loved being at the gym but I could sense a shift; a definite animosity coming from our partner's wife, Marla. It became obvious that a storm was brewing. I'd notice Dave and Marla talking in a corner then they'd walk away when they saw me coming. She'd also disappear into his office, shutting the door behind her. If I brought up how strange I thought this was to Dave he would admonish me for my 'evil mind'. I felt that my world was about to shatter. I couldn't face the possibility of becoming a single mother again.

Although I didn't want to leave the security of my business and all the people I had come to love, I began to bring more and more of my work home with me. Dave and I were friends with so many people in the community: doctors, lawyers, laborers, business owners. We knew them all. I was part of something wonderful and I didn't know how I could possibly give it up, or if I did, where I would go?

Since Elizabeth's settlement, I periodically asked Dave to show me the document with my name on the house we had secured for Elizabeth's equity. He'd flash it quickly in front of me then stuff it back into his lock box. I never felt like I saw the document well enough to really see it so one day I asked if I could take a good look at it. Dave refused. I got a sick feeling that he'd been lying all along about what he'd done with Elizabeth's money. "Show me the money," I demanded.

Dave turned to me with daggers in his eyes. "I don't owe Elizabeth a dime. I've been her father for four years."

Those two sentences cracked my block of denial in two. Elizabeth's settlement should have been enough to let her breeze through college financially and not have to take time away from her studies to work. Under Dave's guidance, however, she was up to her eyeballs in student loans and working at a convenience store in a dangerous part of the city. The only other money she had to live on was the child support I sent her from Ron.

The more I stood up for myself, the angrier Dave got. His threats became routine. He let me know, during every argument we had that he would leave me with nothing; no home, no job and no children. I believed him. Dave was charismatic. He had a following. He was a local athletic hero who traded favors with people in the community for gym memberships. Although he had his share of enemies, they were mostly what he would consider "lower" people whom he had screwed over. Most of the powerful people Dave knew loved him, even though he was playing them just as much as he was playing me.

I finally stopped performing my role as Dave's submissive Stepford wife when I realized that he had always told me what to believe, what to feel and what to think. I can only compare my last year of marriage with him to the movie *Gaslight*. Dave would swear that he didn't say what I heard, didn't do what I saw, and accused me of the very behaviors that he was exhibiting. I began to feel like I was going crazy. What I didn't realize, at the time, was that my husband was systematically building his case against me.

Donna Buiso

Chapter 3

CRAZY MAKING

I increasingly began to wonder where the gentle, caring man I'd fallen in love with had gone. Dave had none of the concern he'd shown me during the very beginning of our relationship. In fact, after the birth of our children, he was cold and distant. His callousness reached new heights when we had a blood drive at our gym. As owners of the gym, Dave and I both felt we should lead the drive by being the first to donate our blood. Shortly afterwards, I received a letter from the Red Cross telling me to see my physician immediately. My blood had been contaminated with the Hep-C virus. I'd had a brief fling with drugs in my youth; a pillow-talk revelation that Dave would later use against me. I was very shaken up but got little consolation from my husband. I could have been telling him about the weather for all his concern. After my diagnosis, Dave quickly got himself tested to make sure he hadn't contracted Hep-C from me. He got the 'all clear' and never mentioned it again even though I was devastated. My doctor suggested that I get my blood tested every six months to closely monitor the virus.

During the year before we separated, the handwriting was on the wall, although I could barely see it. There was one night when Dave didn't come home after we had an argument. There was no phone call or message from him all night. I was home alone with our four and six-year-olds and I didn't know if he was dead or alive. As upsetting as this had been Elizabeth's graduation was coming up and we presented as the perfect family.

Elizabeth's college graduation was a milestone I will never forget. My pride in her was beyond words. All those years later, I still felt that sense of awe I had of her when she was born. . We celebrated with Dave's family and of course Dave was the loving father and husband we all believed him to be. No one would have guessed that anything was amiss in our marriage.

A few months before Amy's fifth birthday Dave announced that he had to stay at a friend's empty summerhouse to 'clear his head'. I had more than a gut feeling that it had something to do with Marla, who did nothing to hide her relationship with my husband. Every place we went she turned up. From the County Fair to the Figawi Ball she was always just steps behind us. I had defended Dave against the rumors, saying that while he might cheat on me, he'd never betray another man like that. I confronted him with indisputable facts but he turned the argument into a tirade against me, trying to make me believe that I was crazy. I asked our business partner if he knew what was going on but Dave had even convinced him that he was just good friends with his wife.

January 1993

Amy's fifth birthday fell on a cold and blustery day in January. The darkness of the day could not overshadow the excitement the children and I had about our planned celebration at the gym. It was a great place for a party, with lots of courts to play on and plenty of room for all her friends. Amy was in heaven. She was the star of the day. Even Evan was exhilarated.

We arrived home from the party exhausted but satisfied with the awesome day we'd had. We'd barely taken our coats off when Dave asked us all to sit down. He informed me and the children that he was leaving for a while. The news was very upsetting to the children and a complete letdown from the good time we had just had.

Amy had shared a ritual with her father. She would get up very early, around 5 am, then go into the back room of the house to be with Dave while he got ready for his day. Those early mornings were the most she saw of him and it devastated her when their routine ended. After he left us, it ripped my heart out to hear her walk around the house at 5 am looking for him. She'd return to her room in tears. I would bring her into bed with me and cuddle her. She never asked me when he was coming back but she repeated the early morning behavior for a few weeks.

Witnessing her grief made me commit myself to trying to save my marriage. I asked Dave to go into counseling with me and he surprisingly agreed. In retrospect, like many 'nice' things he did, I realize now that it was just for show. What I had hoped would help us turned out to be disastrous for me. The therapist loved Dave and sided with him on every issue, even after I told her that I had no idea what our financial state was regarding the business and that my husband refused to tell me anything. I would explain that Dave and Marla made my life miserable at our business, which was where I also worked out. Her suggestion was that I find a different place to work out. I felt that she contributed to the crazy-making cycle.

The more I tried to let Dave know that my family was my priority, above all else, the angrier he got with me. His anger was so irrational that I felt it must be just another part of the long pattern of insanity. In between his outbursts of rage, Dave would do something loving, like taking me in his arms and telling me how much he wanted to fix things. My desire to believe him kept me invested in the marriage. One minute he loved me and wanted to save our marriage, the next minute he was spewing hatred at me. I later learned that this is a process of abuse called Crazy Making.

One afternoon, as I was leaving to take the children to see my parents, I asked Dave if I could borrow his cell phone. The trip was a three hour drive and the weather forecast wasn't good. He replied that he needed it for business but not to worry, I'd be fine. I had a sinking feeling in my stomach because I suspected that Dave and Marla relied on their cell phones to keep in touch with each other. I brushed this thought aside when I saw him give the children goodbye hugs. He then turned to me and gave me a tight, loving hug and a kiss.

"I know things have been rough, but I promise that while you're gone I'm going to do a lot of soul searching and figure out how to save this marriage," he told me. "Call me when you get there."

I hugged him back and drove away feeling some hope that things would get better. I did as he'd asked and called him from my parents' house. In contrast to the loving man I left, I was greeted with him bellowing at me, "What do you want? I'm busy. I don't have time for your B-shit. Don't bother me again."

I tried to remind him of what he'd said while standing in our driveway. "You're crazy!" he'd screamed.

I could hear Marla in the background although I couldn't make out what she was saying. "Stay out there with your crazy mother. I don't want any part of you. Never have. If you call again I will hang up on you." There was more but it became a blur. I hung up the phone incredulous, unable to wrap my head around what was happening. I knew I had to shake it off. Elizabeth was now planning to marry her boyfriend Sam so I had to maintain my composure.

After my brief visit with my parents I returned to Oceanside to assist Elizabeth with wedding plans. I remember feeling numb as I walked through bridal shops with her and discussed menu plans. Although Ron was now in Elizabeth's life, inviting him to the wedding wasn't even a consideration. Elizabeth and I both knew that Dave would be angry at us for even suggesting it.

Later that year, Dave was the proud stepdad who walked Elizabeth down the aisle. Her wedding was beautiful and Dave was the model of family harmony. At the reception, he hugged my family, embraced me on the dance floor and held me close as he whispered in my ear that he loved me. Elizabeth and I danced the 'father and daughter' dance. We held each other and cried as Helen Redy sang "You and Me Against the World", a song about a single mother and her child. When Elizabeth was a little girl, and the song came on the radio, I'd sing the words out loud then at the end I would say (along with Helen Redy) "I love you baby." Elizabeth would reply with the small voice on the recording, "I love you too, Mommy." We'd always squeeze each other afterward. The wedding guests who knew of our past struggles watched us and cried too. I noticed Dave watching without emotion.

After the reception, we hosted a party in the lounge at our gym. After the festivities wound down, and I was saying my goodbyes I glanced around to look for Dave. He had disappeared. I'd seen him at various times during the celebration off in a corner on his cell phone and was fairly certain that he was talking to Marla. He returned home in the wee hours of the morning and quietly climbed into bed with me. I was too exhausted and emotionally drained after watching my beloved daughter get married to question or argue with him.

Before we formally separated, Dave moved in and out of our home three times, putting me and the children on an emotional roller coaster. I never knew from one minute to the next what he was really feeling.

There was one particular day when he was being exceptionally loving to me on the phone. He told me to put the children to bed early and to buy a bottle of wine. He said after the children were asleep we'd talk and try to resolve things. I remember the hope I had in my heart after that conversation. I did what he said, like I always did.

Dave came to the house around the children's bedtime and went into their rooms to say goodnight. He then proceeded to leave. I stopped him and asked what he was doing.

He looked at me, surprised. "I'm leaving. What do you think I'm doing?"

I reminded him about our previous conversation.

"You are completely crazy. I never said any of that. I have no desire to reconcile with you. I never loved you and I certainly don't love you now! Look at you! What the hell is there to love?"

I started to cry. Crying always seemed to empower him and the more I cried the meaner he got.

Dave continued to tell me how crazy I was and that he had never intended to stay and why would he? How could he want to spend time with someone so unlovable? It only escalated from there. By the time he was done with me I was a blubbering mess. I went outside and sat on the hood of his car.

If there was a crazy part of me it was the part that actually wanted him to stay after all the abuse. In Al-Anon it's called "going to the hardware store for milk." I kept thinking that he would remember the conversation from earlier in the day. Instead, he got in his car and called the police.

The officers arrived to see a woman crying hysterically and a perfectly calm man standing with his arms folded and shaking his head in disbelief at his 'crazy' wife. They gently suggested that I go inside. I dragged my emotionally exhausted body into the house and watched from the dining room sliders as they talked to my husband. I couldn't hear what they were saying but they all seemed to be in agreement.

Dave was very calm and used a lot of hand gestures as the police just stood and nodded their heads. After about ten minutes the police and Dave all shook hands and proceeded to get into their cars. I watched tearfully as they drove away, wondering what the hell had just happened.

Dave was still denying any affair with Marla and insisting that he still wanted to work things out between us. This didn't stop him from going to probate court to get an order for specific visitation times with the children over the holidays. I was shocked because he'd given me no indication that he was planning to do this. We hadn't talked about it and he had no reason to believe that I would keep the kids from him. In the court order he had specifically requested certain times on Christmas Eve with the children, and certain times on Christmas day. As shocked as I was that he felt he had to do this, I agreed to his wishes.

My parents drove three hours from Western Mass to Oceanside to spend Christmas Eve with me and the children. Dave had spent Christmas Eve day with the kids and was supposed to bring the children home in time to visit with their grandparents. He returned them late. I was furious because my parents had planned on leaving Christmas Day. I was initially relieved when Dave's car finally pulled into the driveway. We fully expected to begin our festivities with the children.

Evan rushed into the house first with tears streaming down his face. I asked him why in the world he was so upset and he started screaming at me, "Why won't you let Dad be here for Christmas?"

"Evan, I never said Dad couldn't be here."

He was inconsolable, convinced that I had hurt his father deeply. The times on the court order were the times that Dave had chosen. I was so angry that he'd hurt our seven-year-old son like that on Christmas Eve. I looked out the window and noticed that Dave was still sitting in his car in the driveway so I stormed out and got in the passenger seat.

"What the hell are you doing?" I demanded.

Dave started verbally abusing me with the same repetitious words he always used. "You're crazy! You're a horrible mother! You don't deserve anything. You repulse me and always have. I will take those children from you. You will have nothing when I'm done with you. You will return to the heap I found you in!"

He pulled out of the driveway, yelling at me all the time. I was crying and before I knew it we were sitting in the parking lot of the police station which was only minutes from our home. Dave went inside and the same man who was screaming, red in the face and pointing his finger in my face seconds earlier was now calmly talking to a police officer.

The officer came out and asked me to get out of the car. He then escorted me to a cruiser to drive me home. I asked him why I was being driven home in a cruiser. The officer replied, "Dave's just looking out for you. He's afraid of what you might do in your state of mind."

The cruiser pulled into my driveway and I could see the puzzled look on my parents' faces as they peered out of the window. I was bombarded with questions when I walked in the door. I calmly told them that it was another incident with Dave, but assured them everything was fine now and not to worry. The children were already in their PJs and half asleep when I went into kiss them goodnight. I prayed they would be dreaming of Christmas and presents.

Many similar crazy making incidents happened, but one of the worst incidents was one that made me begin to contemplate leaving Oceanside forever.

My friend, Jane, was my rock and had supported me through much of the crazy making. We were so close that I had worn her wedding dress to my wedding. Jane let me cry, helped me with the children, took me to lunch and generally was my best friend. She was always telling me stories of seeing Dave out with Marla or of other people seeing them together. She told me one day that she'd had enough and asked if I would mind if she confronted him. I was grateful for her help so I agreed.

Jane called Dave and arranged to meet him for an early dinner. She promised to call me as soon as she got home to let me know how things went. Her call never came. I tried calling her. Finally she answered the phone and was absolutely hostile towards me. "Yes, your husband is cheating on you, and you deserve it!!" She hung up.

I was stunned. The same man who had consistently denied the cheating was suddenly confessing to my best friend but somehow he'd made it justifiable. I felt sucker punched.

I called Dave at the gym right away. He was surprisingly sweet on the phone and told me not to be upset.

"Come down to the gym. We'll talk and straighten this out," he said in a soft, kind voice.

Once again, I was baited. I drove to the gym and went straight into the office. Dave hugged me, saying that he was glad I came.

"There's a racquetball tournament going on so I have to check on things, but I'll be right back," he told me in a warm, loving voice.

I waited and waited in the office for him. I'd just lost my best friend and I couldn't imagine what he could possibly have said to Jane to make her turn on me. I was in shock, my mind racing with possibilities. After 45 minutes I went to find him.

Dave was sitting with friends in the lounge drinking beer. He saw me and said "Go back to the office, I'll be right there. I promise, honey."

I paced the floor and glanced at my watch as I tried to make sense of everything. I couldn't imagine he would ask me to come if he had no intention of talking to me. I waited another half hour before I realized that he had no intention of talking to me. Once again I found him drinking beer in the lounge, still laughing with his friends. After the horrible shock from Jane and now being ignored so blatantly, I was overcome with frustration. I stomped up to him and knocked his beer bottle over. It wasn't full enough to even make a mess.

"What the hell?" Dave jumped up and grabbed me by the arm then half dragged me out of the gym.

I'm sure to the people he was drinking with that I looked like the crazy wife. I could see it in their eyes. That's when I realized what he was really trying to accomplish. I *was* the crazy wife, and Dave was creating situations where my craziness would be witnessed by others.

Once in the parking lot he let loose on me.

"You are such an embarrassment," he raged. "You're a fool. People think you're insane." He stared at me with pure hatred in his eyes.

Despite my efforts to push him away Dave shoved me into the passenger's seat of his car through the driver's side door. I could feel that I was on the verge of snapping. His voice was all-consuming as he verbally abused me all the way home.

After he screeched into our driveway, Dave leaned over me to open my door then he kicked me out of his car. I tumbled to the ground like a bag of trash. He sped away before I could even catch my breath. My scream came from the very depths of my despair. I couldn't take it anymore. A neighbor called the police and the rescue squad arrived within minutes to take me to the ER. I tried to explain what had happened but no-one would listen to me. I had completely fallen into Dave's trap and looked to the world like a woman losing her sanity.

This was a turning point for me.

A doctor at the hospital recommended I see a counselor, Cindy, whom I now believe saved my life. I told her everything. She calmly listened to me then very gently suggested that I call for an intake appointment at Independence House, a resource center for battered women who are trying to improve their situation. I was shocked because I'd always considered battering to be physical beatings. She explained that people can be abused emotionally and financially too. Dave had pushed me, slapped me, poked me and got in my face, but he had never actually beaten me. I was desperate enough, however, to take her up on her suggestion and called the number on the card she handed me.

Between the individual counseling with Cindy and group sessions at I.H., I began to speak about the hot and cold, kind and cruel behavior of Dave and I recognized the sabotage and financial abuse that he was deeply engaging in. I shared how Dave had hugged me and the children one day, but then he'd walked out the door when he knew I was sick with a raging fever the next day. Instead of helping me, he'd told me to 'deal with it' as he'd complained about how pathetic I was. I listened as the others in the group told similar stories and felt like we were all married to the same person.

February, 1994

I stopped by our gym one evening hoping to catch up with a woman who was in a food co-op with me, planning to return our order book with my order in it. I rarely went to the gym at night because of the children, but as I expected to only be a few minutes I let them play in the nursery while I looked for my friend to quickly hand over the book.

As soon as I walked into the lobby I was met with dirty looks from Marla. She blew out her breath as she sauntered past me in her thong leotard. I saw that Dave was playing racquetball on our glass court on the left wall of the lobby and watched as Marla threw him a knowing glance before walking upstairs.

I followed her into the office where I noted that I could see how irritated she was.

"Marla, the gym is as much my business as yours. I have a right to be here." I reminded her that we were both employees.

"We don't want you here," she replied. "Leave right now or I'll call down to the lobby and have them get Dave off the racquetball court to come upstairs."

I did not move as she called my husband.

Dave stormed into the office and glared at me. Marla stood tall with a smug grin on her face.

"She's bothering me, Dave, and she won't leave. Please call the police and have her removed."

Dave had an opportunity to 'flex his muscles' for Marla. She loved to see him bully me and he loved to bully me for her. "I don't need your crazy ass in my place of business. Get the hell out of here, now, or I will call the cops," he said as he positioned himself in front of Marla.

I stood my ground as I tried to ignore the smirk on Marla's face. "What in the world could you possibly tell them to make them remove me from my own gym?"

"I'm the owner and manager," he replied. "I'll tell them that you and your insanity are disrupting business."

"Your children are in the nursery downstairs! Do you really want to scare them?"

"You have one last chance to get your pitiful body out of here before I dial the phone."

I could not find it in myself to walk away like a whipped dog. I glared at him as he picked up the phone and asked the police to respond to a disturbance at the gym.

In no time at all the police arrived and told me to walk out of the building with them. I explained that I'd done nothing wrong but one of the officers replied, "Sorry Ma'am. The acting manager called us with a problem. We're just doing our jobs."

"I have to get my children out of the nursery first," I said as we walked through the lobby under the curious gaze of a few confused members.

The children spotted the police immediately and looked terrified. "Mommy, what did you do?" they cried.

Not knowing how to answer them I just told them it was all a misunderstanding and that everything would be okay once we got home.

It was only a few days later when I received a copy of the following letter from Dave's lawyer, the same lawyer who at the gym had repeatedly tried to lure me into an affair with him, even though we were both married. This was the beginning of the official threats of Dave taking my children and questioning my sanity.

EXHIBIT A: Copy of letter from Dave's lawyer to my lawyer

LAW OFFICES

APROFESSIONAL ASSOCIATION

MASSACHUSETTS

February 8, 1994

, Esquire
Main Street
Re: v.

Dear Ms. █████████ :

I have met with my client today because of an incident involving your client last night; it seems that around 7:00 p.m. last evening, your client arrived at the health club with the ████ children and proceeded to cause a scene in front of the children and many members. This is in violation of the stipulation presently on file in the ██████ Family Court. Based upon my client's information, I am preparing a contempt action which will be filed immediately. If your client stays out of the Health Club, I will agree to a continuance of the case once we have a date. If she persists, however, I will go forward and subpoena the police officer who was called and any witnesses who were present. You should be aware that during this incident, Ms. █████ followed ███████ and ██████ around yelling things at them in front of all present. She constantly referred to ██████ as a "pig" and dared ██████ to call the police, which he eventually had to do. Then, the children were upset because they were fearful that the police would put their mother in jail.

All of this type of behavior by Ms. ██████ causes me to question her sanity and competence as a mother and for this reason my client and are discussing the possibility of a custody action. If he feels that she cannot handle the children properly, he is prepared to request a psychiatric exam of himself and your client as well as request the appointment of guardian ad litem for the children. Matters appear to be getting out of hand, which also brings me to your last letter.

Mr. ██████ is prepared to show that the counselor presently seeing your client and the children has a female bias, and is known by her peers for this flaw. In fact, her sign reads female counseling. Because of this fatal quirk in her personality, Ms. ██████ lashed out at Mr. ██████ in his session with her in the presence of his children. My client has enough sense to know that this is unprofessional behavior and told her so, thus he will not pay for her counseling sessions for the children. Mr. ██████ has always been willing to accept financial responsibility for unbiased professional counseling for his family. We are prepared to furnish names of several acceptable counselors.

Next, your client complains about timeliness of visitation: My client replies that he is on time in arriving and constantly finds that the children are not ready for him. On a few occasions, he has returned the children between 20 and 30 minutes late (around 6:20 to 6:30) but for very valid reasons, such as the completion of a meal or drying off after swimming. Those have been his reasons. Your client's emotionalism may be the reasons for her complaints about this.

Finally, as for the assets: the motorcycle is worth about $300.00 which ███████ forgot, and the computer was bought by my client for ████████. It is now at the Health Club and is worth about $700.00. If you require an amendment to our financial statement for these items, I will request the same of your client to include all jewelry, furniture, appliances, etc., which she feels are her property. In my opinion, this is all rather petty, especially when you realize that my client has been giving your client additional money totaling at least $1,200.00 since the date of the stipulation.

This case will continue to fester until Ms. ██████ is able to let go and get on with her life. I hope you will be able to point her in the right direction.

Very truly yours,

████████████████

RNR:srr

There was no stipulation that restricted me from going to the gym, which was my place of employment, and I never once called Marla a 'pig'. Also, there was no jewelry and no money given to me. The claims in this letter were completely fabricated but the paper trail that would later be used against me in court had begun.

At the beginning of our marital breakdown Dave had become a volunteer reader for Evan's second grade class. What might have appeared to be a generous gesture was really just one more rouse for him to try cement his reputation as good father. The day after the incident at the gym, when he showed up at Evan's school to read, Evan's teacher had told Dave to leave. She then called me to explain that Evan had gone to school traumatized after his father had called the police on 'us'. Dave wasn't allowed to read for the class again.

The financial abuse that was just beginning was a whole new nightmare. For the past 13 years I had only worked at our gym but once Dave decided to fire me, that was no longer an option. Our situation was desperate. All of a sudden I was expected to keep up the same household on a third of the income. I didn't have enough money for food, my car kept breaking down and was still unpaid for, the water heater broke and I didn't know where to turn for help. Dave had also dropped the health insurance on me and the children. With no way to pay out of pocket, I went on a health regime that consisted of natural foods and herbs to prevent further deterioration to my liver.

I called Dave but he just screamed at me to 'get a job!' Evan was in second grade and Amy was in half day kindergarten, but I did get a part time job in the card shop near our home. As it only paid minimum wage there was no way I could afford babysitters. Whenever I asked Dave to watch the kids, he'd conveniently 'forget' just as I was about to leave for work. What burned all the more in my gut was that Dave was staying at a beautiful condo in the elite town of Snobsville, where he was golfing and having all his bills paid through our business.

Foreclosure notices started to arrive in the mail. I asked Dave what was going on with the house. He refused to tell me anything. Evidently he'd stopped paying the mortgage. I called my father for advice and was stunned to learn that shortly after we were married, Dave had bragged to him that his plan was not to pay the mortgage, to let the house go to foreclosure, and then buy it back with a 'straw'. I confronted Dave about this but he refused to discuss it with me.

One weekend, I decided I needed a break and went to visit my childhood friend Bonnie, who lived in New Hampshire. Elizabeth and her husband were staying with me at the time so they agreed to watch Amy and Evan while I was away. I remember speaking to Dave the first night I was in New Hampshire.

"What are you doing up there? Is anyone with you and Bonnie?" he'd asked me.

In my delusion I took this as a sign that he stilled cared about me and I held on to that delusion throughout the weekend. On my way home from New Hampshire I stopped off to visit my mother-in-law. She loved me dearly and I felt the same way about her. She had been having some physical problems, as well as depression, and I wanted her to know that I still cared about her. A few weeks later she was hospitalized but Dave and his father wouldn't allow me to see her before she passed away.

Dave was emotionless, even at her funeral. As he gave his mother's eulogy he smirked as he glanced in my direction before he listed all the people she had loved: husband, children, son-in-law and friends, being careful to leave me out. My last memory of my mother-in-law was of me standing below her on her staircase as she made her way up to her bedroom. She'd hugged me and said "No matter what happens, you are my daughter and always will be."

In my absence, reality was playing itself out back home. Elizabeth got very sick with the flu. While she lay in bed, her twenty-something-year-old husband was left in charge of the children. Dave apparently swung by and saw the sink full of dishes, garbage out on the back deck and seized his opportunity. Elizabeth later told me that he had left and then come back with a camera to take pictures of the messy house. She also caught him rummaging through my personal things. I began to wonder what his next plan would be and why he felt the need to document what was going on in my absence.

My first and foremost thought was to protect the children. I started to feel like I was in a drowning boat with nowhere left to turn. Cindy was the only person I felt sane around. Everyone else was fast becoming part of the insanity. Dave went to people I was close to and offered them a different reason for why our marriage was disintegrating. Of course it was always my fault.

He told my neat freak father-in-law that after working all day he'd come home to an extremely messy house. My father-in-law tried to tell me how much this bothered his son. "You know, D, my son works so hard. It gives him peace to come home to a clean house. It is very hard for him to relax when he has to step over toys when he walks in the door." I was speechless. I tried to focus on what he was saying because except for toys being around the house was clean and neat.

Then there was my Dad, who always wanted more affection from my mother. Dave told him that after working all day he'd come home to a cold wife. My Dad sat me down, looked me in the eyes and tried to tell me how much it would mean to Dave if I could just be more affectionate. "D, I can't tell you what it would mean to me to come home and have your mother put her arms around me. Dave is feeling the same way. It would go a long way if you just kiss him on the cheek when he comes home and show concern for the day he might have had." I thought of all the times I had done just that and tried to tell my Dad that. He insisted that Dave felt I just wasn't affectionate enough with him.

One of our friends had a wife who was even more 'Stepford' than me. He suggested that if I contributed more to the household it would improve my relationship with Dave who, apparently, felt over burdened by responsibility. But it was when Elizabeth asked me to be more understanding of Dave's 'platonic' relationship with Marla that I began to see how calculating his intentions really were. "Mom, they are just friends and co-workers! Why are you so suspicious? Dave said he would never ever cheat on you but you are always accusing him of things." Elizabeth scolded me.

Everyone asked me to change something about myself for Dave. Once again I questioned my sanity. Only this time I was in therapy. My counselor helped me realize that all of the things Dave was saying were not true, however, I was starting to feel the underlying fear of just how dangerous Dave was. His strategy was clever and calculating.

I thanked God for Cindy. She helped me to realize that I wasn't crazy, bad, or inadequate, but that I was at the mercy of an extremely manipulative and abusive man who was systematically isolating me from my entire support system, which included my best friend and my family. Things finally started to make sense.

I'd often thought of going underground, but with no connections and no money I saw no way out. This is when I first thought about moving away. I never thought I'd leave my beloved home, Elizabeth, or Oceanside but the foreclosure notices and the constant abuse of me and the children were taking its toll. I was continually getting sick and weakened so much that I could barely get out of bed on some days. I recognized that I was falling into a true clinical depression.

I spoke to my physician who put me on a mild anti-depressant. I weaned myself off the pills in less than a year. Of course Dave would use my depression as a reason to make me look like an unstable mother in our future court proceedings.

I had to get a job but I didn't want to try and work where Dave could sabotage any job I might find. The pain of being excluded from everything that was so dear to me was overwhelming. Dave was no longer hiding his relationship with Marla and they had become the new "Mom and Pop" at the gym. Elizabeth realized this and she was horrified. "Mom, I'm so sorry. I look back and I see how he manipulated me. He is so believable!"

As his threats to take the children became more frequent, Elizabeth composed a letter to present to the court should Dave act on his threats of getting custody of Evan and Amy.

EXHIBIT B: Letter of Support from Elizabeth

To whom it may concern,

I wish to write this letter in support of my mother, ███████ ██████.

My mother brought me up as a single parent. I have only lately, as an adult, realized how poor we were growing up. I had no idea because my mother never let me go without. I took dance lessons, played softball and went on school trips with all the other kids.

My mother read to me, sang to me, taught me piano and brought me to the beach so we could spend quality time together.

My mother's priority was always me, and it's the same with my siblings. I have always felt loved and cared for and see the same intentions with ███ and ███.

Elizabeth

The counseling sessions with Cindy were one of my few support resources I had in Oceanside, but they were enough to give me the strength to do something about my situation. I began to make plans to move back to my hometown in Western Massachusetts. I had absolutely no money and would be leaving Oceanside like a refugee, but I knew I had to go.

I told Dave that I was leaving and he was furious. He'd made it impossible for me to stay but was so beside himself that I was going that he went to court and filed a motion to prevent me from leaving. It was the only time the court ruled in my favor. The judge, however, sternly reprimanded me for taking the children out of school in the middle of the year.

After his court motion fell through, Dave's threats and bullying did not prevent me from planning to leave. He had consistently threatened to take the children from me even before he left the household and Cindy knew better than I did that he meant to follow through.

She felt so strongly about it that she wrote a letter for the court for me to use in what she believed would be inevitable future litigation.

EXHIBIT C: Letter of Support from my counselor

Psychological Services
Cindy Barg, MED.

1994

To Whom This May Concern:

███████████ has been my client for the last year and a half. She came to me as a result of trying to work out her marriage and resolve personal issues in her life.

███████████ first came to me on antidepressants as she was suffering from depression. Over time and extensive sessions in therapy it was discovered that she was also suffering from emotional abuse.

Unfortunately, given the nature of emotional abuse it is elusive in nature simply because the wounds are not visibly tangible to the naked eye. However, the cycle of emotional abuse leaves its scars internally, therefore making it very difficult to understand how any individual can be devastatingly affected by it.

There is much discussion about domestic violence in the form of physical abuse. To define what emotional abuse is becomes ambiguous simply because its validity is always questioned. It is true that abuse is not restricted to the gender. Historically, and to date, it is culturally sanctioned for men to be angry. However, if a woman shows anger, other consequences precipitate and labels like aggressive, uncontrollable and unfit are often used to describe her nature. My focus here is to point out that despite ██████'s past over twenty years ago with drug abuse, she was still suffering from the affects of emotional abuse. She was also a victim as a child. Yet, today, she has broken the cycle and she has worked extensively on bettering herself and her family and her past should be no reflection on her competency as a dedicated and committed parent.

It is in my opinion and in utmost respect and high regard that Ms. ██████ is an extremely bright and gifted individual with tremendous insight. She is a devoted mother who has struggled out of past emotional trauma. Her children ██████ and ██████, are very loved and well taken care of by their mother.

It is also in my documentation after counseling ██████'s husband, ████████████, that he is extremely emotionally abusive and he falls in the batter's characterization of denial, (rage) and control through intimidation and lies and screaming intentionally in front of Ms. ██████ to scare her and to make her feel minimized. It is important to note that Mr. ██████'s behavior toward his wife affects the children greatly and in the long run the cycle of abuse he displays to his wife presently will have a very profound effect on the children. And when he intentionally emotionally abuses her, he is also abusing his children.

In conclusion, Ms. ██████ is an extremely competent parent. She has devoted herself to choose a life that will promote emotional well-being not only to herself, but to her children as well. She had the courage to leave a very painful marriage, despite the tremendous loss she has undergone through all of it and the only way to break any abusive cycle is to get out of it. Simply for that, it is very important for me to state that she is also giving her children a gift.

Sincerely,
Cindy Barg, MED

Dave was eventually left with only one way to attack me - through our children. Amy and Evan were six and seven years old. Their anxieties about moving had been exacerbated by Dave who had filled them with fears about leaving Oceanside. As young as they were, he tried to make them believe that they had the power to make me change my mind. They had many visitations with him that ended with them coming home very upset because Dave had told them that they wouldn't see their friends, nor him, nor take swimming or tennis lessons, and God only knows what else. I told them that when their Dad started talking to them about these things to please tell him it made them uncomfortable. These were the days when I still believed that he had some concern for them.

As hard as it was to see the children hurting, they were going to hurt no matter what I did, or where we were. It was truly a no-win situation. Some women flee a relationship to save their lives because of physical beatings. I was fleeing to save my life from the emotional beatings. Not only did I have the looming foreclosure and Dave's continual abuse to contend with, but my health had deteriorated and I began to feel like I was dying inside.

By the time I'd put the move together I was seeing things differently. I remember sitting across from Dave one day, discussing the move, when I noticed his eyes were as cold and mean as any I've ever seen. It felt like he was boring holes through me with his eyes as he stared right through me. I got a chill up my back as I began to believe that he could have actually had me killed if I'd stayed. He would justify it as he always did with "it's just business." He would never do it himself, but I had no doubt that if he felt he could get away with it, he would have hired someone to take me out. As a precaution, I went to the police departments in Oceanside and in the town I was moving to and alerted them that if anything happened to me they should take a very close look at my soon-to-be ex-husband.

Dave told everyone we knew how awful I was for taking his children away from him. Some members from our gym stopped talking to me. I loved our business and thought of its members as family. It hurt so much to see them turn their backs on me. There were a few members who realized what was really going on and they made an effort to be supportive of me. Dave viewed their loyalty to me as an act of war and made their lives miserable by bad mouthing them and discouraging their gym memberships.

One of these members felt so compelled to voice his thoughts about my situation that he wrote the following letter to be used in support of me, should Dave try to take my children.

EXHIBIT D: Letter of support from Bill H.

█████████

9/25/94

To whom it may concern:

I have known both ████████ & ██████ for ten years on a personal basis. ████████ has been nothing but a fine, honest and upstanding individual, caring and always having an interest in people while being a devoted family person. She has always done whatever was right for her children and makes sure they are cared for in the proper manner.

Having known ██████ at the same time, I have seen him, in many cases, outright lie to people, and in (some) cases lie to the point of parlaying the lie into something illegal. I have seen him (be) dishonest while putting on a very convincing front that the other person was in the wrong. He is a manipulator extraordinaire. I have seen his children many times not with him, but (being) taken care of by someone else when in his possession.

If there is any question of character, ██████ is the person who would sacrifice what is necessary to take care of her children so that they would grow up to be well-adjusted adults.

Sincerely,

Bill ████████

Before I left Oceanside I approached one of our business associates who had assisted us with the financials of the gym. When I asked him about the state of our finances, he had deflected my questions by saying that Dave had told him I'd kicked him out of the house and was keeping him away from his children. He was shocked to hear my version of events and admitted that he was also unclear about what Dave was doing with the business financials. I couldn't wait to drive over the bridge and get away from Dave's web of lies.

After I found a place to live in Western Massachusetts my mother agreed to help me with the rent. A few days after Christmas, I rented a truck and loaded it up with essentials, which included my piano. Without looking back, or shedding a tear, I left my beloved home, my ocean, Elizabeth and my friends. Just as someone leaves a war-torn country with their focus only on the few steps in front of them, with no regard for how they'll manage after their escape, I left Oceanside with my focus solely on finding relief from the hell that I had been going through for the past couple of years.

Chapter 4

THE MOVE

January, 1995

I left my town in Oceanside after twenty-three years of calling it home and believing that I would die there. My beloved house had been everything I'd ever wanted: a backyard deck; a garden with compost area and rhododendron bushes; the finished basement that meant comfort for kids, teenagers, and guests; the peacefulness of our dead-end street. Looking back, I can't believe that I left with no emotion at all beyond my determination to escape my husband's reach.

I drove into my hometown of Rolling Hills and was overwhelmed by my deep sense of relief. I could breathe again. HE wasn't nearby, and HE didn't know any of my friends in Western Massachusetts. Dave couldn't just walk into my home. He couldn't get in my face and give me that look, or call me names, or stick his finger in my face and push or threaten me anymore. I felt like I had been let out of prison. As the New Year approached, I felt hopeful of a new beginning for me and the children.

We had barely settled into our new home when Dave decided to throw Amy a huge birthday party at the gym. He invited all her old classmates and made sure that she had something to miss when she returned to Western Mass. Still, I remained optimistic, focusing on the future and knowing that I needed a divorce.

My lawyer, Joe King, made many promises. He obtained a court order requiring that Dave pay our first and last month's rent as well as security deposit in lieu of the fact that we were forced to move because of the looming foreclosure. I took cash advances on my credit card to pay for the move, sure that I would be able to pay it back when Dave reimbursed me. Dave didn't honor the order so the debt ended up following me around for years.

My lawyer also told me that we'd be having a trial and assured me that he didn't want me to leave the marriage empty handed. He also was sure the court wouldn't allow me to leave with nothing. With renewed hope I again focused on the future in my new environment.

My cute duplex apartment was a little white house with a big back yard on a dead end street, just up the hill from the elementary school that I'd attended. The inside was small but Amy and Evan had big bedrooms while I had the smallest one. I took only my bed and the couch we had in our basement. I bought the children used bunk beds, which they were excited about. It was also close to my parents. Being three hours away from them had always been a good thing for me, but now I desperately needed their help. They were not hugely supportive, but did agree to help me by watching the children as soon as I could get a job.

My first night in my new apartment was unforgettable. It was MINE! The thrill at seeing my name on the lease and the utility bills empowered me even more. I felt I had an identity for the first time in years. It had been so long since I'd had an identity other than DW. The relief I felt was enormous. I knew, however, that I wasn't off the hook yet, not by a long shot.

Dave still had ties to our children which gave him ties to me. It quickly became clear that he was prepared to use them at every opportunity to get back at me. I felt I had left the battlefield only to send my children back in to the war.

I got a job as a bank teller within the first week of moving. I felt so hopeful and renewed. My first day started out full of excitement. I brought the children to school and intended to head straight to the bank, a short distance away. After taking Evan to his third grade class I walked Amy to her first grade classroom. Amy was always so quiet and independent. I thought back to her first day of kindergarten. I'd expected her to cling to me like her brother had done. Instead, she'd made herself right at home and when she'd noticed me hovering had asked "Are you still here?"

This time was different. Amy did not want me to leave her. She became hysterical and wrapped her arms and legs around me. She cried and begged me not to go. "Mommy, please, please don't go. Please!" I wanted to just hold her and comfort her.

I was used to Evan acting out, but not Amy. She'd been through so much change and now she needed me. I felt guilty for the lack of consistency in their young lives. The conflict inside me was overwhelming. I kept glancing at the clock, knowing that if I showed up late for my first day that it might be my last day.

The teacher called the school counselor and he literally had to pry my baby from me so that I could leave. The vision of him pulling her off of me, her arms outstretched toward me, the sound of her crying out to me, "Mommy don't go!!!" is burned into my memory forever. As I walked down the hall and out the door I could still hear her screaming for me.

I wanted to sit in the car and cry until I had no tears left, but I had to compose myself and stuff every painful feeling and thought that was flooding my being deep into my belly. I was still shaken when I arrived at work but I put on the best face that I could. I did have to tell my new boss that I'd had a hard time dropping my children off at school, but I tried to make it sound less disturbing than it really was.

Lance, the school counselor at Evan's new school, called me in for a conference. He told me that he suspected that my son was being abused. At first, Lance didn't suspect Dave. Evan had mentioned things to Lance about Marla's oldest child, a boy about four years older than Evan. I admitted I had overheard my children talking to each other about this boy hitting them and swearing at them. I knew Dave and Marla often left Evan and Amy in his care. Lance showed me a letter he'd written to Dave expressing his suspicion that Evan was being abused by Marla's son. Lance asked me to deliver the letter to Dave at his next visitation.

The next time I turned the children over to Dave I handed him the letter. He read it in front of me and I watched as his face turned beat red and his muscles tensed in anger. He stared at me as he ripped it up. He then embarked on a campaign to discredit Lance and tried to have him fired. As Lance got to know Dave better, he developed a whole new concern for the children. His concern was shared with me when Lance handed me literature on sociopathic behavior. He wasn't ready to report to DSS although he felt if more information came about he would have to do his 'mandated reporting'.

I also took the children to a counseling agency in town. Although Dave knew that I had a life threatening condition and had to have my blood tested every six months, he never resumed the court-ordered health insurance after we left Oceanside. I was thankful to find an agency that worked on a sliding scale.

After Evan's first visit with the agency counselor, Tracy, she called me into the room and sent Evan out into the hallway. Tracy told me that she was going to have to file a report with DSS in response to what Evan had told her, including how his father made him vacuum and hit him in the head if he didn't do it right. I was so relieved that someone was finally going to do something to help my son.

On the next visit, however, Tracy said that she'd talked to her supervisor who'd advised that because Evan didn't have any bruises there would be no proof of abuse.

March 1995

While with their father, Evan and Amy were thrown together with Marla's children so that Dave and Marla could do their own thing without the kids. The youngest four children were left way too often with Marla's oldest son, which was far too much responsibility for a young boy. Generally, Marla's girls were spoiled and Amy was tolerated. The boys were pretty much ignored unless Evan was targeted by Dave and Marla. The girls' birthdays were always huge events while Evan's were barely acknowledged. The one exception was his ninth birthday.

Dave was aware that Evan was having a hard time making friends in his third grade class. The children were not kind to him and made fun of him for being the new kid. He had left everything familiar only to be rejected in his new surroundings. My heart was in a constant state of ache for him. Evan's art work from school expressed how much he missed being in Oceanside. I noticed that he often mentioned his friends and his old home, but never his father. I asked Dave to help me throw a birthday bash for Evan similar to the one he'd put on for Amy two months earlier.

I wanted the party to be held in our new town so that Evan could make friends. Dave refused. He did, however, organize a party at his gym, inviting all of Evan's friends from his last three grades. It was the last time he did anything special for Evan's birthdays until years later. I realized Dave's motive when it became apparent that after Evan had a ball at the party, it was excruciating for him to leave his old friends and return to the school that was so unwelcoming to him.

Working at the bank was not what I would have chosen for work, but it was pleasant. I enjoyed working with money and I liked interacting with the staff and customers, but my income was not even close to what I needed to support myself and my two children. Although child support had been court ordered, it rarely came. Whenever the Massachusetts Department of Revenue (DOR) notified Dave about his arrears he'd throw me a small bone, just enough to keep the DOR off his back. Then it would be months of no payments until the DOR chased him up again. In the meantime, I scraped to make whatever income I could. I would occasionally ask Dave for help, but it never came.

Dave had a woman working for him at the gym who had three granddaughters on whom she lavished clothes. She would pass on the second hand items to Amy. Dave, however, forbade Amy from bringing these clothes home. He only allowed her to wear them when she was with him. The same thing happened when I asked Dave to buy Evan a pair of sneakers. Evan was only allowed to wear them when with his father.

I took a second job bartending in a local restaurant a few nights a week to supplement my income. It was the last thing I wanted to do. I'd worked so many years in restaurants as a young mother that I could never have imagined returning to it. My first restaurant job in Western Mass was at a Mafia owned establishment. My boss would literally snap his fingers at me. It felt belittling and demeaning and I hated being there. For the time being, however, I didn't believe I had a choice. I had two small children at home who depended on me for everything. I couldn't wait to leave work and go home to try and recapture those fleeting feelings of hope and freedom that I'd first felt after our move.

I was scheduled to work a few nights a week but my boss would think nothing of telling me the night before that he wanted me to work an extra shift the next day. He never asked. He just told me, and there was never any expectation that I might decline. I made up my mind to leave as soon as possible.

The children were in school when I was at the bank. My parents only had to pick them up and babysit them for a short time until I got home. On the nights that I worked at the bar I was able to feed Evan and Amy then get them ready for bed before I left. My children were used to being active so those first six months without their usual after-school activities were difficult for them. Summer neared and I had to make a decision about quitting one of my jobs because I wouldn't leave the kids with my parents all day.

I decided that restaurant work was the more lucrative and quit the bank and went to work full time in another restaurant. I worked late into the night and was on my feet for a constant eight hours. I would then get up early with the children to get them off to school. Sometimes my feet ached as soon as they hit the floor but that job freed me up to be with my children and be active in their lives. I volunteered at their school and participated in their activities, on some days driving back and forth between opposite sides of town to bring Evan to football then Amy to gymnastics.

At night, after they'd completed their school work, they'd have their baths and then we'd enjoy a little cuddle time. I cherish those memories of our snuggling up in my bed; the three of us watching Nick at Night. It was the best part of my life.

Amy went to bed first. We'd read, talk and look up at the same glow-in-the-dark stars on her walls and ceiling that she'd had in her bedroom in Seaville. I'd bought her a book of children's meditations and I would let her pick one every night that we would do together. Sometimes it would be an ocean theme or maybe a visualization in the woods that would put us in a peaceful calm to end the day. One of Amy's favorite things to do as I cuddled with her was have me write on her back and see if she could guess what I was writing. Then she'd do the same to me, writing endearing things like "I love you" or "You're the best!"

After Amy was settled with a tight hug and a kiss on the forehead, I'd spend time with Evan. Our routine was similar, but he had a particular request that always seemed to relax him enough to fall asleep. I'd have him close his eyes then I would start with his toes and put every toe "to sleep" by saying "your baby toe is so relaxed and is melting into the mattress." By the time I got to the top of his head he would be sound asleep. He'd ask me to do this almost nightly. It felt so good to be able to do something that helped him experience some peace.

This peace was shattered when Evan began to experience night terrors after visiting with his father. I'd wake up to hear him run screaming out of his bedroom hours after he'd gone to bed. I was so afraid he was going to hurt himself as he charged around the house and bolted up and down the stairs. I'd have to grab him and soothe him until he calmed down enough for me put him back to bed. He would be fine for a few nights but then the terrors would start again. I kept holding out hope that someone would eventually do something to help my children.

How foolish I was to think that three hours driving distance between me and Dave would make a difference in our lives. I had mistakenly believed that he wouldn't bother with his visitations. He'd been so involved with Marla and her children that he'd barely noticed his own. Even when we still lived in Eastern Mass., the children were consistently left with friends and members of his staff while they were supposed to be in his care. I was surprised when he faithfully upheld his visitation rights, although I soon realized it wasn't for the noble reasons I had hoped.

I had agreed to meet Dave every other weekend in a town that was the half-way point for us both for delivery and pick up of the children. I would bring them to the designated spot. Dave would greet us, then immediately launch a verbal attack on Evan.

"Why isn't your hair brushed? It doesn't look like you brushed your teeth. Are you chewing your nails again? How about standing up straight for a change?" he would barb at him.

Watching this scenario every single time we met was unbearable. I just wanted to put my children back in my car and speed away. The pit in my stomach became a knot that refused to unravel for hours after I returned home.

When it was time to pick up the children, I'd wait an indeterminate amount of time for Dave to arrive at our meeting place. Cell phones were not common back then. I'd have to use a pay phone to call people to see if they knew if or when Dave had left Oceanside. Sometimes I'd spend a few hours sitting in my car feeling anxious, wondering if he would ever show up. Ironically, I talked to someone in Oceanside who said how frustrated Dave was that he always had to wait for me!

Dave would eventually show up and he'd act as though it was a continuation of the Friday drop off. I could see him yelling at Evan as he pulled into the parking lot, Evan's head dropped to his chest in response to his father's angry face and flailing arms. My son would emerge from the car with a tear stained face and Amy looked afraid to breathe. Although my insides were churning, I was grateful to be taking them home and tried to appear cheerful as they climbed in my car.

Evan saved his anger at his father for me and Amy. As soon as he got into the car he'd start acting out.

"Amy you are SO stupid! Mom, change the channel!" he'd scream.

At home, Evan refused to bathe or to brush his teeth. He'd kick the walls and scream about how much he hated Dave's girlfriend Marla.

I'd ask the children general things about their weekend. Did they have fun? Did they see their friends or go to the beach? They would both clam up and offer nothing. I had no doubt that they were instructed to keep silent.

Dave rarely came out to Western Mass. to see the children but the couple of times that he did were horrific. The first time was right after we moved, once he realized that I'd taken the lawn mower. He had kept possession of the motorcycle, 21 foot aqua sport boat and our home, yet he was furious enough to drive six hours, round trip, to repossess the lawn mower.

I'd learned to pick my battles and this wasn't one I was prepared to fight so I agreed. In my urgent departure from Seaville, I had forgotten to grab the photograph albums from the storage space in the basement that contained photos of Amy and Evan's baby and toddler years. I had taken a copious amount of pictures and painstakingly put them in order. I asked Dave if he could please bring me some of these photo albums. He replied, "Hell no. You're gone and will never see another thing you left behind." He saw the children for only a few seconds before he headed back to Oceanside, leaving them hurt and confused.

On Dave's next trip he came for Amy's dance recital. A few days earlier, my daughter Elizabeth had also driven out for the recital which turned out to be a five hour long event. It was a few hours into the recital before Amy would come on stage. Evan was getting very bored and fidgety. Dave promised him that if he would be patient he'd take him and Amy to a place in town called the Kid's Zone where kids could bounce, climb and tumble. Evan loved this place and did his best to endure the two hours before his sister came on.

Amy joined us after her performance and told her father she wanted to stay and watch the end of the recital so she could watch her friends. He agreed so we all stayed. It was his weekend and I knew trying to take Evan myself would have caused an uproar. My poor Evan endured five hours of little girls in tutus while he waited to go to his favorite place.

The recital finally ended and Evan jumped up and down excitedly, "Yeah Amy! Guess where we're going now?"

His father looked at him, "Sorry, it's too late," he sternly shot at Evan.

Evan deflated like a balloon. As we all walked out to the parking lot, Evan mumbled under his breath, "Stupid Amy." Dave overheard the remark and exploded. "What did you say? What did you say?" He kept repeating this while he dragged Evan over to his van with Amy running behind. I watched him shove Evan into the passenger's seat and Evan's head hang low as Dave screamed at him with flailing arms.

I told Elizabeth I couldn't let Evan go with him. I went over to the van and leaned in the window. "Please, Dave. Let Evan drive with Elizabeth and me."

Dave's response was, "Back away from the van or I will run you over."

Before I could open my mouth again he pulled away with me trying to hold on to the door handle of the passenger side. He was still screaming at Evan while Amy sheepishly cowered in the back seat.

Elizabeth and I returned to my apartment. She was as upset as I was. Dave stopped by so the children could pick up some overnight things to stay with him in the motel room he'd rented for the night. We watched as the van pulled up in front of the house and Evan and Amy literally ran in and out of the house to get their stuff without saying a word. Neither child even looked at me or Elizabeth as they sped past us without acknowledgement. After they left, Elizabeth and I lamented about how helpless we both felt and how scared we were for the children.

During our first summer in Western Mass I drove the children to Oceanside to visit Elizabeth. We met her at her apartment and after lots of hugs, kisses, and "I miss yous" we settled down to chat while the children played with her dogs. We would have been content to stay with her but it was Dave's weekend and I had to turn the children over to him.

Elizabeth and I drove the children to the gym to meet Dave. As we walked into the foyer Dave came to greet us. Amy ran to him and begged him to take her and Evan out on his boat and to bring me and Elizabeth with them. He agreed. I was surprised but up for anything that might make things better for my children.

Dave had a little dingy that he would let the kids 'ride the wake' in. Amy loved it but Evan didn't. His school counselor had told me that Evan had a fear of open water. Amy couldn't wait to ride in the dingy and I watched her scream with delight as we pulled her behind the boat. Evan didn't want to go in it but his father egged him on. "Come on Evan! What are you afraid of? Didn't you see how much your sister loved it? She's not afraid so why are you?"

Evan got into the dingy. Dave had taught the children hand signals to let him know whether to go faster or slower - thumbs up, faster - thumbs down, slow down. Evan was gripping the dingy tightly and as the boat started to rev up he quickly did a thumbs down. Dave started to laugh and put the pedal to the metal.

Evan looked terrified as he tried to hold on while continuing to give his thumbs down. "SLOW DOWN!!!" I screamed, afraid that even though Evan wore a life vest he'd panic even more than he was already if he fell into the water.

Dave screamed back at me, "You're overreacting, as usual," and then began to laugh sadistically as he watched me getting increasingly upset. I realized at that time that he got his kicks out of watching his terrified son, and even more by watching me suffer for him. It was at this point that I realized the lengths he would go to hurt the children, and to hurt me.

Later that summer, I again drove the children to Oceanside for their visitation with Dave. I was so homesick for the ocean, and even more so for my beautiful daughter, Elizabeth. We had always been so close and it was difficult living so far from her. She made frequent trips out to see us and, whenever I could, I'd try to arrange to visit her.

Once we arrived, the children expressed that they didn't want to spend the whole weekend with their father but wanted to spend some time with their big sister and her husband. Elizabeth knew that Dave was in a tennis tournament and didn't think it would be an issue for the children to sleep over at her house on their first night while he was busy. She took the children over to the Tennis Club to talk to Dave about what they wanted to do. I went to the mall.

As I was shopping, I looked up to see a visibly upset Elizabeth rushing towards me.

"Thank God I found you," she cried! "You've got to go to the Tennis Club and pick up the kids, right away. Evan mentioned that he wanted to come spend the night with me and Dave flipped out. He started screaming at him and pushing his finger in his face. I left Evan literally cowering in the bushes."

I told Elizabeth to go home and said I would meet her there. I ran to my car and drove the short distance to the Tennis Club.

Dave was out on the court playing tennis and Marla was watching him from the observation window. My two children were sitting by her looking like scared statues. I grabbed them by their hands and began to leave. Marla started to swear at me and protested my taking them.

As I drove to Elizabeth's house Evan kept saying, "It's my fault. It's my fault. Dad is going to be sooo mad at me."

He was literally shaking. I was shaking too. I knew the backlash of taking the children on 'his time' would be severe but it was a chance I had to take. It also made me more and more apprehensive about what was going on when I was three hours away. I wondered if it was worse because I was there, or was it always this way for the children when they visited with their father? We tried our best to enjoy our night with Elizabeth, her husband and her dogs, although we were apprehensive about any more possible incidents that night or the next day. Thankfully there weren't any and with relief we left early in the morning and drove back to Rolling Hills.

In October I traveled back to Oceanside for what I believed was going to be a divorce trial. I had been in touch with my lawyer days before our divorce date but when I arrived at the court house I could not find him. My lawyer rushed to my side just as Dave and I were called into the courtroom to appear before Judge Hatcher with no explanation of why he was so late. Judge Hatcher began the proceedings with, "So the only issue before us today is the reduction of child support."

I couldn't believe my ears. "I can't live on what he's supposed to send now," I protested. "I have nothing and two small children to care for. Please, your honor. Dave has our boat. Make him sell that if he needs money, but please don't take my child support."

Dave's lawyer then beseeched the Judge. "Your honor, my client only keeps the boat because he knows how much his children enjoy it when they visit him."

Judge Hatcher leaned down toward me and asked "Mrs. A. Do the children enjoy the boat?"

I knew I was dead in the water. I turned to my attorney, who would not look at me, and then I looked back to the judge. "I was supposed to have a trial today!"

My lawyer calmly looked straight at the judge and informed him that he could not do a trial because he had other things on his agenda. He also startled me by referring to a meeting that he'd had with Dave and his lawyer, of which I was totally unaware. I refused to agree to a lesser amount of child support.

The judge called a recess.

My lawyer took me into the hall. "This judge is not in your corner. If you argue this he's likely to take more from you," he warned.

I felt sick inside and didn't know what to do or where to turn. Again, my naivety was astounding. We went back into the court room where I agreed to a lesser amount of child support but only if and after Dave resumed our health insurance.

I left the courtroom to find that my lawyer had taken off faster than speeding light. He never brought up the court order, which was supposed to reimburse me for my moving expenses. My only consolation was that the judge left the 'division of assets' open. However, when I later received my divorce decree it said that everything was settled. It didn't even resemble what had transpired in court and had been written up by Dave's attorney.

I drove back to my new home dazed but thankful to be far away from this insanity. My lawyer didn't return my many phone calls but did send me a disheartening letter, four months later.

EXHIBIT E: Letter from my attorney

LAW OFFICE

 AND

PROFESSIONAL BUILDING

BLUE HILL AVENUE, ████ MASSACHUSETTS ████

February 21, 1996

Ms. ████

, Massachusetts ████

RE: DIVORCE STATUS

Dear ████,

Thank you for your letter dated January 10, 1996 relative to the status of your divorce.

You refer to information on your divorce status and from what I can learn is that a judgment nisi of divorce will be entered for you, as plaintiff, upon receipt of a separation agreement signed by both parties.

Enclosed please find the separation agreement as prepared by the office of ███████. The first seven pages are "boiler plate" reproductions and are usually found in every agreement, whereas the following six pages (Exhibits A - F) are more meaningful.

As I read the exhibits, they do not resemble nor conform to any understanding that I can recollect.

By his own admission by offering to pay $300.00 per week child support, he must earn $1,000.00 per week or more and he expects that three (3) people to live on 1/3 of that and he has 2/3 of it for himself.

It was my understanding that the distribution of marital assets would not be determined at the time of the divorce but would remain open. We were further led to believe that he was impecunious; lost all his worldly possessions and was filing a petition to be declared bankrupt. Apparently this is not the case and he has misled everyone, including the Court.

By virtue of the wording contained in Exhibit "A: he continues to be prospering in the various business enterprises that you and he started together. He referred to the remaining residential property as the "former marital premises" and one wonders what the status is of that home today.

As you know our office did a voluminous amount of work on your case and the costs, expenses and sanctions far exceeded any emolument received, but that is not our problem. What concerns me was the inability to discover hard core evidence of the life style, mode or manner of living and financial status of your estranged husband.

There seems to be no doubt that he is clever, sharp and a superb manipulator of things, property and people. It is most perplexing, confusing and embarrassing to be unable to delineate Mr. ███████ with any degree of accuracy. His business relationships with ███████, ███████ and ███████ are a state of the art and most bewildering to any persons of ordinary intelligence.

It is unconscionable for Mr. ███████ to attempt to relegate, banish and exile you while he reigns over all of the property, as Lord of the Manor.

What he did to your daughter was as mean and despicable act as anyone could ever do and he should be richly awarded for it.

Attorney ███████ has been calling quite frequently and this may be an omen that Mr. ██████ is about to embark upon a new venture of some nature, but needs a divorce to accomplish the same.

We will communicate with Attorney ████████ and inform him that the agreement has been forwarded to you for your comments and advises.

Kindly inform me of your intention relative to the agreement and your response to this communication.

Truly yours,

████████JNK/lr

I never signed the agreement that was sent to me but my divorce was finalized anyway. I did not have funds to hire another lawyer and fight this. Besides, as upsetting as my divorce was, I had more important things to deal with. There was no doubt in my mind that abuse and neglect was continuing during the kids' bi-monthly visitations with their father, but the children told me next to nothing. Every so often, however, something would leak out that gave me clues as to what may be going on. The children and I were watching a show one night on TV in which the father was being cruel to his son. Evan mumbled under his breath, "He's just like Dad." Another time, Evan mentioned to me that Dad only liked girls, not boys. One night, as I was putting Amy to bed, she told me that her brother shouldn't go anymore with their father because Dad was "so mean to him."

Amy also shared an incident where Evan and one of Marla's daughters had been racing to the car. Evan had collided with her and she'd fallen. Dave had punished Evan by not allowing him to speak for the rest of the day. I asked Evan about this and he confirmed it. He said at one point he'd tried to whisper something to Amy and Marla had caught him and called out to Dave "He's talking! I heard him!" Evan was locked in the bathroom as punishment.

I felt helpless because I couldn't protect Evan or Amy. When they told me of another disturbing event I couldn't believe my ears. I think they shared this because they didn't they realize the danger they'd been in.

Dave's girlfriend had dropped her youngest two children and my children off at the barn where she stalled her horses. The youngest being Amy, who was only seven, and the oldest was probably eleven at the time. My children were not used to being around horses and apparently there had been no one around to supervise them. They told me that they were left out in the rain. Eventually they had to urinate so they wandered off to "pee in the woods." I questioned their father about this and he yelled "Once again you're overreacting! There was a caretaker on the property that they could have gone to in an emergency! What they do when they are with me in none of your business!"

I later found out that Dave scolded Evan for relaying this story to me. Evan said that if he hadn't said he'd wanted chicken for dinner that night Marla wouldn't have had to leave them at the barn to go shopping for the chicken.

My unhappy boy became increasingly out of control and fought me at every turn about everything from food to clothes. He began to get nasty with Amy by verbally putting her down at every opportunity. They were both obviously in severe pain and I was frantic to help. The school counselor was a Godsend to me. Lance took Evan under his wing and spent a lot of time helping me to understand what was going on. He was very concerned about my children and we brainstormed a lot about what to do. We also talked about the possibility of Evan self-medicating in the future with drugs and/or alcohol if we couldn't get him help. I brought up the possibility of involving DSS but Lance said he still didn't want to go that route. He'd had a lot of frustration in dealing with the agency in the past and felt that sometimes it could make things worse for the children. I was at my wits end and feeling increasingly helpless.

Chapter 5

DASHING HOPE

My hopes of things getting better in Western Mass were fading quickly. I tried to keep the children involved in activities that kept their minds on healthy things but as in every area of our lives, Dave often found ways to sabotage us. During our time in Western Mass Amy and Evan had become involved in many activities such as softball, wrestling, Brownies, gymnastics, basketball and football. No matter the importance of the game or event, however, Dave DEMANDED his weekends with his kids.

Evan spent most of his football years in Western Mass on the bench because he simply missed too many practices and games. Amy's Brownie troop had worked for months to save for a big weekend that involved a special trip that happened to fall on Dave's weekend. The troop leader called me several times to bring Amy home early from troop meetings because she was having stomach aches. After initially being so excited, Amy finally told me that she didn't want to go anymore. I tried to question her but she had nothing else to say.

Elizabeth called me to tell me that she'd read in the Oceanside County Times that our marital home was going to auction. "I really think you should be there Mom. You need to find out what Dave does with the house."

Fueled by fury, I shocked Dave by showing up at the auction. He saw me drive up in front of the house and turned on his heels. I stood and watched him talking with two men in suits. Although I was ignored, I stood close enough to hear that everything had been prearranged through the bank. Knowing that it would be illegal to buy his own house back at foreclosure, Dave had arranged for a 'straw' to buy the house on his behalf then to sell the house to my ex father-in-law shortly after. My father had been right to warn me about Dave's plan. I watched, helpless, as the 'straw' bought our house for only $80,000, with a $5,000 deposit.

I thought back to my first lawyer and how one of the first things she wanted to do was to slap a restraining order on Dave to prevent him from doing anything with our assets. At that time, however, Dave was still convincing me that he wanted our marriage to work, urging me to reconsider divorce proceedings. I had believed him and backed off on further litigation. This had given him plenty of time to move his assets around.

After the auction was over and everyone left, I looked at my former home and all the grief that I couldn't feel when I'd first left the house pounded in my chest. I took one last glance over the children's play yard and the area where my garden used to be. My heart ached at the sight of my rhododendrons, which were in full, glorious bloom.

Dave saw the look on my face and came over to me, touched my arm and said, "You know, D, if I or my father ever sell this house, you will get your share."

I looked into his eyes as he stared back at me with that soft look that he could manufacture so easily and, for a split second, I saw the Dave I thought he was so long ago. I actually considered believing him. I quickly came back to reality, however, when it dawned on me that he was just trying to ensure that I wouldn't make an issue out of what I'd witnessed. I drove home in yet another fog of amazement at the depths of Dave's manipulation.

I later learned Dave had set up a deal where he could live in what had been our marital home while his father technically owned it.

Dave rarely showed his face in my town but when he did, he often looked like he was going to jump out of his skin. It wasn't his turf so he didn't have all the familiar people he was used to manipulating around him. He couldn't lie to the school staff the way he had in the kids' former school because they only saw me. If I had nothing else, I had their full support. As much as he tried, Dave's crazy phone calls to the school, complaining about me and the incompetent school counselor, fell on deaf ears.

In spite of our increasing financial hardship, my kids were always fed well and dressed well and I always made sure the children had their extra-curricular activities. They didn't go without, no matter how far behind Dave was in child support, or how many extra hours I had to work.

Evan loved his private violin lessons made possible by a dear friend from my old choir. Amy, my gymnast, had her heart set on going to a gymnastics school called Whip City. She was so good at it and loved it so much that I was determined to make it happen. I wanted her to have the same opportunity to be involved in something she absolutely loved. I jumped at the opportunity to make some extra money when someone at work needed to take two weeks off. I worked every single night and earned the money I needed for her tuition. I was completely and utterly exhausted but elated. The look of joy on Amy's face when she was able to participate in gym meets and flip and tumble at Whip City was priceless to me.

Although we didn't have much money, we always found fun things to do in our area. We lived in farm country and there was always something to enjoy there. A favorite treat was to attend the high school football games. In the fall, we'd visit pumpkin patches and hay mazes. In October, the three of us celebrated Halloween at Riverside (now Six Flags). We had so much fun going on the rides. Towards the end of the night we decided to go on the antique car ride. I'll never forget how frightening it was for Evan and Amy. Ghouls and ghosts kept running up to the car and pretending to try to get in while they made blood curdling screams at us. Both the kids were so frightened they couldn't even speak. The mother bear in me came out and I screamed at the actors and swatted them away from the car. This had been our last ride of the night and we were entirely ready to go home afterwards. As scared as they had been, the kids and I laughed about it all the way home. They teased me about how crazy I'd looked, waving and screaming at the spooks to "Leave them alone! You're scaring them!" Especially because that's what they were supposed to be doing.

Every other weekend, when I had time to myself, I'd go line dancing and two-stepping. I absolutely loved it. I'd meet my friends at a local bar and dance almost the whole night. I'd go home exhausted but happy, but then thoughts of my children would resurrect my fear for them and I'd be unable to get to sleep.

One night, after I collected the children from their weekend visitation with Dave, I noticed Evan scratching the soles of his feet. I know this is a sign of an allergic reaction so I questioned him about what he had to eat and drink that day. Nothing seemed out of the ordinary. He did tell me that Marla had given him a homeopathic remedy. I routinely use alternative remedies and certainly don't have a problem with them. However, Marla was always giving my children 'remedies' that she felt they should have; some of them homemade by her.

Evan didn't know why she gave him the remedy, or what was in it, so I called Dave and explained that Evan was not only scratching but he was breaking out in welts. I asked what was given to him so that I could relay that information to the ER doctors if I needed to take him in.

Dave screamed at me, "It's none of your business what she gave him! Don't call me again with your lunacy. I don't care what's going on, do you hear me?"

There was a blizzard outside. Amy was already tucked up in bed sleeping soundly. I stayed up all night, worrying and watching Evan; prepared to take Amy out of bed if we had to run to the ER. Thankfully, Evan was okay in the morning. The welts went away and the itching was gone but I will never forget the stress of that long night.

Evan had another minor incident a short while later. A friend at work had bought the children a trampoline for Christmas. They were on it all the time. However, Evan ended up hyper-extending his back while jumping on it. We still didn't have health insurance so it was out-of-pocket to take Evan to the doctor. I also had to pay for the x-rays, which was a huge expense on an already strained budget. The doctor said that if Evan didn't feel better after a few days he would have to order more x-rays. I'd completely depleted our finances. I called Dave to ask him to help with his son's medical expenses, which was another of his court ordered obligations. Once again, he screamed at me that once he got the insurance reinstated, "I will never see another penny from him!" He never did help me, nor did he call back to see how Evan was doing.

I had thought things were going to get better once we left Oceanside but they continued to get worse.

Chapter 6

DSS

I was becoming increasingly disturbed by the little I knew about my children's visits with their father. From what I could discern, Evan was constantly being picked on by Dave and Marla and Amy was trying hard to vie for the same attention as Marla's girls.

Evan is an incredibly talented musician and it showed at an early age. Whenever he tried to show off his ability on the trumpet, guitar or violin, Marla would say how much better her son was as a musician. Evan was also told that he was fat and that he didn't brush his teeth enough, which was why they were yellow. Evan wasn't fat, and the dentist told me the slight tinge to his teeth was the result of his taking antibiotics for ear infections when he was younger.

Marla's youngest daughter was treated like a princess. She had to get glasses and Dave and Marla gushed over how beautiful she looked. Amy came back from a visit with them and told me that she needed glasses. I took her to an optometrist where Amy was prescribed mild glasses for reading, but was told not wear them unless it was for that purpose. She tried to wear them all the time. It became an issue between us. I had to hide the glasses because she was convinced they needed to be part of her every day. She couldn't wait to show off her new glasses to her father. I don't think she got the reaction from Dave and Marla that she had hoped for because the glasses became a non-issue pretty quickly after her return.

One weekend, after we'd arrived home from the children's visitation, I heard Evan teasing Amy. What he said in a mocking lilt hit me like a brick, "Amy and her naked video!" I always tried not to press them for information about visits with their dad, but in this case I couldn't let it go. After a lot of coaxing I finally got the story from Amy.

I learned that Amy and Marla's youngest daughter were taking a bath when Dave and Marla went into the bathroom with a video camera. They'd asked Amy to stand up and dance the Macarena. She was naked and didn't want to do it. Dave promised her that they were only filming her from the neck up and that he would never show anyone. That same night, Dave popped the video into the VCR. Marla, all the children (including Marla's teenage son) watched Amy dancing in full frontal nudity. My eight-and-a-half year old daughter was shamed and humiliated.

I had to take the chance of notifying DSS. I didn't know half of what went on at Dave's but what I did know was extremely upsetting. I tried not to imagine the worst, but I had to protect my child. The video, the lack of supervision, and Amy coming home with 'sexy' underwear was too much for me. At the very least, she was being violated emotionally.

After I called DSS and briefly told them my concerns, a social worker showed up at my house. He talked to me and the children as he quietly observed our living conditions and rapport with each other. I told him about the video, about the incident with horses, and the emotional abuse I suspected was going on during their visits with Dave.

It didn't take long for me to hear back from the social worker. "I spoke to your ex-husband and he did admit to the video. However, he promised to not ever show it again and would in fact get rid of it."

"You have got to be kidding!!!" I yelled into the phone.

"The children are in a good home," The DSS worker responded. "If you were the violator it would be more of a problem but as they spend the majority of their time with you we are confident that they are in a safe environment. Should anything similar come up again, please contact us."

Of course this ended up being a backlash on the children. I have no idea what the repercussions were, but I do know that my children came back from visitations even more miserable and were very mad at me for "the trouble I caused" their father.

One year later, a similar incident did come up. Evan returned home in a rage and a depression; the worst I'd witnessed so far. I couldn't get him to talk, nor could the counselor get anything out of him. I was frantic so I called Elizabeth and told her what was going on with her brother. She drove out to Western Massachusetts to help us.

Elizabeth went into Evan's room and stayed with him for quite a while. She came out with a look of consternation on her face as she said, "Mom, we have a dilemma. I do know what's bothering him, but he told me only under the promise that I would not tell his father that he'd talked about it."

She finally explained to me that ten-year-old Evan had watched a very explicit pornographic film. It might have also contained some violence but Evan hadn't gone into much detail. I didn't know what to do. If I contacted DSS and they failed to act on this information God only knows what would happen to Evan. His trust in me and his older sister would be forever broken. If I did nothing, then God only knows what was happening and would continue to happen at their father's house. After much deliberation with Elizabeth I decided to call DSS again.

The same social worker was not working for them anymore. Once again, the social worker who talked to Dave about the incident assured me that Dave had promised not to let such an incident happen again. Dave had claimed that the video belonged to his roommate and Evan had gotten a hold of it. DSS apparently felt that the issue was resolved. Once again, however, Evan got in trouble with Dave for 'opening his big mouth'. The difference this time was just as I feared. Evan felt hugely betrayed and lost his trust in the people who loved him the most.

I was in constant turmoil about what to do. Should I just try to run away with the children? I had no money, no resources and no protection. If Dave found me, he would get the custody he'd always threatened me with and there would be no one to protect my children from him. Should I refuse to send them on their visitations? The answer was always the same; Dave would take me to court on contempt and make sure he got custody of the children.

I started to rethink my decision to remain in Western Mass.

Chapter 7

ANOTHER MOVE

1998

I missed my beautiful daughter, Elizabeth, and my beloved ocean terribly. I'd only left Oceanside because of my need to get away from Dave. However, the three-hour distance between me and Dave wasn't helping. In fact, it was making things worse. I could no longer deny that Dave saw his children as nothing but property and a tool to beat me with. I couldn't stand the fear of wondering what was happening to them when they were with their father and the pain on their faces when they came home was heartbreaking.

My jobs didn't allow me time off for court dates and it was becoming increasingly difficult for me to go back and forth to the Oceanside County Courthouse. I had a jalopy of a car that barely made the visitation trips. I tried to get a change in venue for our case but staff at the Western Mass. court house said this would be near impossible and the only hope would be in a good lawyer to represent me. There just was no money for an attorney, let alone a top notch one that may or may not win. All I wanted was peace for me and my children. After living in Western Mass for three years, I thought about moving back to Oceanside County. As soon as my decision was made, the universe responded.

My landlady, who lived on the other side of the duplex that I rented, was a wonderful, sweet lady who loved my children and me. During the third year of our tenancy, however, she had been killed in a car crash. Her daughters, who inherited the house, did not want to keep it so they promptly listed the property and sold it. The buyer, a young man in his early twenties, had verbally promised the daughters that he would keep me on as a tenant after they expressed concern for me.

After he bought the house, he approached me with a lease that said if I was ever late on the rent (which I never had been) that I would have to pay another $50 a day until it was paid. After I refused to sign it he presented me with an eviction notice. I made phone calls and found out that I could fight it. I also found out that this young man wanted his sister to move into my side of the duplex and was trying to force me out. Although I felt I could have won this in court I didn't want to go through the drama of having to live in the same building with him. I felt the universe was giving me a kick in the butt to make a decision about moving.

I called Dave and told him that the children and I were being evicted and needed to find a place to live. I knew Dave was living with Marla even though he kept our marital home as his legal address. It had become his 'other house': a place for his family to vacation while in Oceanside; a place to keep "HIS" things and a place he could escape whenever he fought with Marla. I suggested that the children and I move back in to our old home. I even offered to pay rent to his father.

"I don't want you there, and my father doesn't want you there," Dave replied.

Here was an opportunity to have his children close by again and yet it seemed he couldn't care less. I explained to him the circumstances of the impending eviction and explained that I did nothing wrong to warrant it. The children and I needed a place to live. It all fell on deaf ears. "I don't care D. You made your bed and now you can lie in it. It's your problem, not mine," he said before hanging up the phone.

I turned to the one person I knew would help me. Elizabeth was anxious to have me and the children return to Oceanside, not only to help us, but for her own personal reasons. She agreed to help us in any way she could.

Elizabeth's marriage to Sam had been brief. Shortly after my move to Western Mass. she and I had shared numerous lengthy phone conversations about her divorce. Now, three years later, we were having even more lengthy phone conversations about her upcoming marriage to her childhood sweetheart, Carl.

Carl had never been married and wanted a big December wedding. As in her first marriage, Evan and Amy were to be in the wedding party. This time, however, so were Elizabeth's young siblings from her biological father, Ron. She had contemplated inviting Dave because she didn't want to hurt Evan or Amy by omitting him and when she asked me my opinion I told her it was a decision she and Carl would have to make and that I didn't want to be held responsible for any decision they came to. I added that I couldn't imagine Dave sitting on the sidelines and watching Ron walk Elizabeth down the aisle.

Elizabeth later told me that she talked to Dave and explained how she and her father Ron weren't comfortable having him at the wedding but if he wanted to stop by the reception he was welcome. He chose not to attend. Elizabeth hadn't had much of a relationship with Dave since before she went to college so his choice not to come was a relief to her.

With Elizabeth embarking on a new life with Carl, she was even more excited about my return to Oceanside and helped me look for a place to live. I was willing to live anywhere in Oceanside County except near our marital home in Seaville. Elizabeth and I discovered the rents were much higher than I was used to paying and could find nothing within my price range but I had an idea.

During one house-hunting trip to Oceanside, I visited the minister at my old church and explained my dilemma. He suggested that I talk to one of the women whom I used to sing with in the choir. She knew a lot of people and had lots of connections. Sure enough, she had a lead and told me of an empty house close to where she lived. It also happened to be three streets away from my former marital home.

Although I didn't want to live in Seaville, I was desperate. I called the owner, who lived in California, and she was very pleasant as she explained that she'd had a bad experience with renters so was now contemplating selling the property. She admitted that her heart wasn't really in letting it go as she'd raised her children in the house and wanted to keep it in the family. Based on my choir friend's recommendation, she was willing to consider me as a tenant.

As she described the house, small with its three bedrooms, a den, a deck and deeded beach rights, I immediately checked it off in my mind as unaffordable. Then she told me what they were asking for rent. I thought I was hearing things when she named the price I was already paying for my duplex. I had to see the house for myself.

I'd agonized about my decision to move but eventually concluded that fate was leading me home. There had to be a reason why, of all the places in Oceanside County, the one house that was perfect in every way was so close to Dave. I'd done so much spiritual work since my separation, devouring books by Wayne Dyer, Deepak Chopra, and others, attending a Spiritualist Church in the city and spending time in meditation. These life lines gave me strength and were helping me to perceive things differently. I began to see this as an opportunity to change something in me that would make things better. I believed that maybe this was an opportunity to improve my relationship with Dave and vowed to work on it.

I rented the house and made a resolution to approach Dave differently, convincing myself that things could be better between us. Another plus to moving back to our old town was that the children could return to a familiar neighborhood and to their old schools. Once again, hope stirred in my heart.

I informed Dave that I would be moving back to Seaville and his reaction surprised me. He was pleasant on the phone and even offered to help me move. Elizabeth had already taken Amy to stay with her before our April 1st move-in day. However, when the time came for me to move, the truck and the help Dave had offered never arrived. I told some customers at work about my dilemma. Without saying a word to me, they rallied together and five wonderful men showed up at my home with a moving van. I was stunned when they announced that they would be volunteering their man power for the day.

The men packed me up, followed me all the way to Oceanside, and moved my things into my new home. I remember Dave pulling up in front of the house. He sat in his car watching and scowling, but never offered to help as the men went in and out of the house, moving my furniture in.

I took my angels out to dinner and let them know I would never forget them or what they had done for me. I hugged each of them goodbye as they boarded the van to go back to Western Mass. I said a silent prayer for the people who came into my life and had become like family to me. People who started out as my customers and touched my heart with their good intentions were a salve to my wounded soul.

Amy was happy to return to Oceanside but Evan did not want to move again. He had finally acclimatized to his new surroundings, made friends and thrived academically. Now in fifth grade, he was enrolled in the Project C program for gifted children who needed more of an academic challenge. It was rigorous program but he still made the honor roll and got his name in the local newspaper for excelling. He was so excited to take this news to his father.

"Dad said my report card was OK but Amy's was even better," he said, his face heavy with dejection.

Evan begged me to let him stay with my brother and his wife so that he could finish out his school year with his friends. They didn't have children of their own and seemed happy to have the experience of having a child in the house. Evan was ecstatic when they agreed. He looked up to my brother as a fellow musician, and was so excited to think about living with him for a while. I didn't want to leave him behind but I knew he needed this. The only problem, as usual, was Dave.

Predictably, Dave had a fit. "I will not allow it. I will fight it. I'm the father and I say it's not going to happen. Period!"

I talked to a lawyer who said I was within my rights as the custodial parent to allow my child to spend a few months with his uncle. I thought it was a done deal until I talked with my brother again.

My brother had always hated Dave after witnessing what I'd gone through, emotionally and financially. He had nothing good to say about him until the day Dave called him up to wield his manipulative powers. Suddenly my brother informed me that unless he had the blessings of BOTH parents, he couldn't follow through with the plan. I asked him how he could honor both parents by giving in to one. He either honored me and Evan, or he honored Dave's wishes. My brother wouldn't budge.

Evan was very upset. I told him I would try again to reason with his uncle. I made arrangements to go to my brother's house to see if we could talk this out. His reaction horrified me when he stood up and bellowed, "Dave loves those children! He told me how much he suffers when he's away from them. He said you walked out on him, that he begged you not to take the children, and now you use them against him and try to punish him just because you think he had an affair."

I couldn't believe it. My brother wouldn't even let me talk. I ran into the bedroom, reeling from the attack. I was sobbing when my sister-in-law came in to console me. My brother came in, grabbed her by the arm and pulled her out of the room.

"Stay away from her!" he yelled.

This was supposed to be about Evan staying with them to finish out his last two months of school. Instead, it got turned on me and once again, the focus was on Dave's accusations against me.

I arrived home and explained to Evan that his uncle wouldn't go against his father's wishes. For the first time in his young life, I saw Evan stand up to his father. He went to the phone and called him.

He was emphatic when he stated. "I want to stay at my uncle's house. If you don't let me, I don't ever want to see you again."

Surprisingly, his father took him seriously and relented.

My relationship with my brother has never been great, but since that incident it has deteriorated. However, once Evan moved in with my brother he got the structure and peace he craved. I will always be grateful for the time my brother and sister-in-law spent with Evan and for the way they cared for my son, gave him chores to do, and checked his homework. I missed him terribly but knew this was so good for him.

My brother took Evan to karate in Western Mass. then enrolled him in a karate summer camp to be held in the next town to me so he Evan could continue the sport after he moved back to Oceanside. It was $600 and my brother said he was willing to put in $200 if his father and I put in $200 each. I found the money for karate and also sent weekly checks to cover Evan's expenses. Dave never paid his share of the karate tuition but my brother didn't seem to care.

Once we were settled in Eastern Mass. Amy and I both missed Evan, but it gave us a chance to have time alone together. I noticed the irony of Dave never calling or seeing Amy except on "his" weekends, even though we were just down the street. I also noticed that Amy didn't call him, nor ask to see him outside of her normal visitation time.

It took me a few months to find a job. I lived on an Earned Income Credit during that time. Just as I had in Western Mass., I picked up any odd jobs I could find. I had one job that literally involved counting cars. I'd sit for hours near an intersection and punch which direction each car was going into a little machine. Although he hadn't paid any child support in months, Dave took Marla on a vacation to Florida.

I took my case to the DOR office in town. They explained what I already knew; that as long as Dave was self-employed and making even meager attempts to pay child support, there was not much they could do except keep track of what he owed. Their figures and mine were consistent until the day I received a letter from the DOR office in Boston. The letter claimed that after conducting an audit, a much lesser amount of support was owed to me than had previously been stated. I immediately called the local DOR office and conveyed my confusion. A woman who had previously worked with me picked up the call and whispered into the phone. "You're right! Call your state rep. immediately but please don't mention my name."

I did call my state representative who then looked into the matter. It wasn't long before I received another letter from the Boston DOR stating that an 'illegal audit' had been done at the DOR office at Oceanside Probate Court and my original amount owed to me had been reinstated. I called the Boston DOR office for an explanation and for the name of the person responsible for the audit but all they would tell me was that the person responsible would be severely reprimanded. I could only imagine that Dave had somehow manipulated a DOR employee at the courthouse. Of course I had no proof, but at this point nothing surprised me about Dave's capabilities of persuasion.

Except for the financial stress and missing Evan, life was peaceful. Amy and I walked the beach and rented movies. I gave her piano lessons and we got closer than ever. The only hard time was the weekends with Dave. As Evan wasn't around, Amy took the brunt of his abuse. She hated Marla, who continually made disparaging remarks to her, always comparing her to Marla's youngest. Amy, who had always been thin, was told "she was getting a little belly" and warned that she shouldn't eat so much. I began to worry that Amy might lean towards anorexia because the remarks bothered her so much.

One Sunday night, when Dave returned Amy to me, he came into the house and began to explain that she was picking up a few things then returning to his house with him. I noticed him burning holes in Amy with his eyes as he talked to me. He was furious with her for not cleaning her room to his satisfaction. Suddenly Amy ran to me and threw her arms around my waist.

"Amy, you know you're a liar!" Dave screamed.

The more she burrowed into me the angrier he got. I told him Amy was staying home.

He began to scream at me. "She needs to go back and clean that room!!!"

I held on to Amy, refusing to acknowledge his demands. He angrily muttered something then left, slamming the door behind him.

In his wake, all my forebodings flooded back to me. I had finally been enjoying some peace. I missed Evan but I knew he was happy at his uncle's house. Amy and I had been happy too, but it was a respite that was short lived.

Chapter 8

THE NIGHTMARE CONTINUES

My brother brought Evan back to Oceanside for Karate Camp around the middle of June. It was only a few miles from our new home and I planned to pick Evan up near the end of the month. It felt so good to have my boy back. The separation had been good for all of us but it was time to have Evan home and resume our new life together.

As I pulled into the camp I saw that Evan looked vulnerable and lost. I'd hoped the camp would give him some sense of strength and security but Evan was fidgety and nervous. I know he was happy to see me by his tight hug but I felt that he had a foreboding about being back in Oceanside. By this time I had found employment at a seasonal restaurant. The hours were long and I was concerned about the inevitability of Evan spending time with his father while I worked.

At first, things went smoothly. We had a beach at the end of our street that was on a beautiful lake. One of our neighbors was a boy Evan had gone to school with and after they met up at the beach it was soon common knowledge that the kids were back in town. They quickly reunited with their old friends and also made new ones.

My birthday is at the end of June. Elizabeth, Evan and Amy were obviously plotting something special but were careful not to leave any hints of what it might be. On the morning of my birthday, Elizabeth approached me with a blindfold. My children all giggled as they made me climb into the back seat of Elizabeth's car while they kept checking my blind fold to make sure I didn't peek. After a very short drive my blindfold was lifted to reveal that we were in a parking lot parked in front of a big ship. The kids all pulled me out of the back seat and excitedly dragged me to the line of passengers waiting to embark. We were going on a whale watch!

The kids all knew how much I loved dolphins and whales and came up with the best of gifts each year. We had a wonderful day together as we hugged, laughed and cried in awe at the magnificent creatures of the sea, enjoying the salt spray on our faces. It was a wonderful day and life was finally feeling good again.

In August, Evan joined a local children's football team. He didn't miss a single practice or game. Whenever he had played football in Western Mass he had been almost invisible, always relegated to the bench. On this team, Evan showed football prowess I never knew he had and quickly became a valued player. . Whenever we'd show up for practice the other kids on the team would be excited to see him.

Marla couldn't bear to see Evan or Amy excel in anything. Their accomplishments were immediately upstaged by one of her children. If Amy got a good report card then she had to show them a better report card from one of her children. If Evan relayed a story of someone telling him what a good musician he was then she would tell them how much better one of her kids was at an instrument.

Evan continued playing trumpet and bass, as he had in Western Mass., and he joined his school band in the fall. Dave and Marla would attend his performances but Marla would always make it a point to arrive late and then make remarks about how she was there to see someone else performing in the band.

One of the most heartless incidents of emotional abuse from Dave occurred just after the death of Evan's favorite teacher. I know that this teacher always treated Evan lovingly and with respect and she'd helped to make his adjustment to a new class much easier for him.

Upon hearing of her passing, Dave had insisted on taking Evan to her memorial service. I was uneasy about his eagerness but Evan seemed grateful that his father was taking an interest. As I sat wondering how Evan was bearing up at the service I heard a car pull up in the driveway. Surprised to see Dave dropping Evan off so early, I knew as soon as I saw Evan walk in the house that something awful had happened. "What's wrong honey?" I asked.

"Dad made us leave because he said he saw me biting my nails," he snapped back at me as he flew up the stairs to his room.

I followed him.

"I wasn't biting my nails, Mom. He kept saying he caught me but I wasn't!" he cried. "Evan, even if you were it would be understandable. Someone you cared about just passed away and that's got to make you feel so sad," I said as I tried unsuccessfully to console him.

The abuse was constant. The incidents with Evan were becoming almost seamless and he barely had time to recover before Dave would attack him again.

Things began to get very scary after this. It was shortly after his teacher died that Evan's grades plummeted. Although he wasn't flunking out, he wasn't doing the excellent work he'd been doing before. Dave used this to humiliate him. He never offered to work with him or get him a tutor. Instead he chose to shame him.

Both Evan and Amy told me of an incident that happened while they were out to dinner with Dave and Marla. Apparently, Marla had told Evan that he had always been an F student. Evan replied "I never get F's." Marla then pulled out her son's report card and waved it in front of Evan and told him to "read it and weep."

My poor Evan would tell me these things with such bitterness for a young boy. He took all of the remarks to heart, which was obvious by the pain on his face. Evan hated Marla and expressed it to me regularly. I'd fight my feelings of helplessness and try to help Evan work through his feelings. "Evan, you're a great kid. You're a great musician and you're smart and funny. Please don't pay attention to what Marla says. I know it hurts you when she says these things but just don't believe them," I'd say, doing my best to encourage him as I watched him biting his nails. Eventually Evan did become an "F student"

Looking back, I can see how Evan fulfilled all Dave and Marla's expectations. They told him he was an "F student" so he became one. They told him he was a 'bad kid' so he acted like one. He was accused of drinking and doing drugs before he actually did them. They never encouraged him or made him feel good about anything that he did. It was torturous to watch this and to see Evan becoming chronically angry again. The more his father shamed and humiliated him, the worse Evan's grades and behavior became. The more his grades slipped, the worse his father treated him. I felt powerless to counteract this vicious cycle.

The children came home one day all excited. "Papa (their paternal grandfather) says he's taking Dad, us, Auntie Dee, Uncle Rick, and Cousin Mickey to Disney World in January!" Evan squealed with delight. A few weeks before the event was to happen, however, it was canceled. I was alone in the car with Amy while driving her to a friend's house when she told me the news. Dejected, Amy angrily told me, "It's all Evan's fault."

"What did Evan have to do with it?" I was incredulous.

"Papa said he had to cancel the trip because Evan's grades were so bad."

I told her that I didn't believe for a minute that Evan was the reason for the canceled trip. I knew that with all the reservations and plans that had gone into it there was no way my ex-father-in-law would have lost all that money just to teach Evan a lesson.

As soon as I saw Evan I told him just that. However, not only did his sister blame him but so did his father, grandfather, aunt and uncle. I could tell by his face that no amount of talking was going to convince him otherwise. I later found out that the cancellation had something to do with botched reservations and the trip was postponed, not canceled.

The end of the football season was another opportunity for Dave to make Evan feel awful about what should have been a happy time of celebration. For the end-of-season banquet Elizabeth asked Dave if she could go as his guest so he would not bring the treacherous Marla. He agreed. We all sat at the same table as each child was called up to the stage to receive a trophy and a jacket. At the end of the evening the first comment that Dave had for Evan was "You had to be the slowest walking kid in the building." I didn't hear it but Elizabeth did and she told me in disgust after seeing the now familiar dropping of Evan's head in despair.

Music is what kept Evan going. He was never far from his guitar and whatever instrument he could get his hands on. Dave and Marla went to see Evan in a concert with the school jazz band. Elizabeth went with me. Evan was excellent and it was joyful to watch him doing something he loved so much and was so good at. As we went to congratulate him after his performance, Dave quickly walked over to him to admonish him about him having a laser pen in his pocket.

I'm not sure why it bothered Dave or why it was more important than encouraging or praising his son. As Elizabeth said, "Does he come just so he can always make Evan feel negative?"

The following year, seemingly out of the blue, Evan refused to go to football practice. Surprised, I questioned him about it. "I don't want to go, ever again." He refused to give me any explanation. Amy practiced cheer leading at the same field the football team practiced on. After I dropped her off I went to talk to the football coach. I explained that Evan didn't want to come to football anymore and asked if he had any idea why. The coach told me that Dave had asked him to make Evan run extra laps and do extra pushups because his grades were bad. The coach had told Dave it wasn't his place to discipline Evan outside of football and at practice he was well behaved and obedient. Up to that point he'd been proud of himself in football and had loved the camaraderie of his team.

Dave was irate when he found out that Evan had quit football and threatened Evan with everything he could think of to force him back to practice, including taking away his musical instruments. At one point, he locked everything up that Evan had left at his house, including his guitar. Dave knew that Evan's music was his lifeline. All the counselors and professionals agreed that taking Evan's music away from him had no productive effect whatsoever and would, in fact, have the opposite effect. This did not stop Dave from using it, repeatedly. I went to go to court to get an ex-parte motion for Dave to return Evan's belongings. My request was granted but ignored by Dave.

It was becoming increasingly unbearable for Evan to visit his father. As I was getting ready to leave for work one evening, Evan said he refused to go with his father. Dave called me and angrily asked me if he could come into my home and physically remove Evan. I emphatically said no. I wasn't comfortable leaving Evan home alone at that time of night. I also was terrified by what might transpire between Dave and Evan if Evan let him into the house or if Dave lured him outside. Once again I was in the nightmare of choosing between losing my job or protecting my children. I called in sick.

By November, my job was winding down for the season. Amy confided in me that she was glad I was going to be home more because she did not like spending so much time with her father. She said she hated Marla. She added that Marla's youngest daughter was the 'star' of the children and privileged in every way.

Around Christmas time, Dave took Marla, her youngest daughter and Amy to the Sugar Plum Fairy Ball. It was a big event. Dave rented a tuxedo and the girls all dressed in gowns and high heels. This was Dave's weekend with the children and although Evan wasn't included in the outing he was forced to spend the evening at Marla's house by himself. He wanted to stay home with me but our protests to Dave went unheeded. Evan had to endure listening all weekend to everyone else babble about the fun and excitement they'd had at the Ball without him.

Evan came home very unhappy and asked me if I knew how sometimes people pretended to be mean but were really kidding. He said, "Dad says he's kidding, but he's really, really mean."

I knew he was talking about the 'hostile humor' Dave so often used; he would degrade and shame then say "I'm only kidding. Can't you take a joke?" I explained 'hostile humor' to Evan, hoping he'd understand his father often used it with me, and with others, as well as with him. I think Evan understood what I was talking about but was unable to detach from his hurt feelings in spite of understanding.

It appeared that any big event, like Christmas, was an opportunity for Dave's cruelty to flourish. It was common for him to give the children checks for gifts. The checks often bounced so he'd take them back to 'hold on to them,' which meant the kids never did get their money. It was also common for Dave to promise to pay the kids for work they did at the gym and then not pay them. Amy told me that her father owed her money for babysitting at the Gym. "Amy, did you try asking him for the money that he owes you?" I asked her. She answered, "Yes, but he reminded me that he took me out to lunch the week before. Mom I didn't even want to go to lunch that day."

Evan tried asking his father for some of the money that was owed to him so he could buy Christmas gifts. Dave flatly denied owing him anything. However, a few days before Christmas Dave dropped Amy home and told her to send Evan out to the car. Evan came back inside and told me that his father told him he asked Amy to send him out so he could give him some of the money he owed him. Evan opened his palm and showed me the dime his father had shoved into his hand. He looked at me with eyes that were filled with a combination of pain, anger and sadness. All I could say to him was "I'm so sorry, Evan." I tried to hug him but he pulled away screaming "I hate him!! I hate him!!!!' as he ran up the stairs and slammed the door to his room.

The situation between Evan and his father got rapidly scarier and uglier. Evan told me that one night his father had pulled him out of bed screaming at him that he hadn't brushed his teeth. Evan said Dave was manhandling him so he fought back. As he told me this story I had a flash-back to when my mother-in-law was alive. During our visits with her, when Evan was just three or four years old, Dave would scream and berate him for no reason that we could see. My mother-in-law and I would beg Dave to stop, to no avail.

Evan began to go to his father's house with a jackknife in his pocket. I saw it sticking out of his pants pocket and I took it from him. He quickly cried, "Mom I need that for protection! Dad puts his face in mine and pushes me against the wall. Sometimes he pushes me down on the couch and gets on top of me!" I was at my wits end trying to figure out what to do.

Evan would find excuses not to go to his father's but eventually Dave would lure him back by talking like the Dad that Evan wanted. "I miss you Evan. We're all going to see the Blue Man Group. Don't you want to come?" Dave would implore him. Although Evan would take the bait the visit would usually result in another abusive incident. It never ceased to amaze me how Evan always held out hope for a different outcome. I would then remember how the same thing had happened to me a few years earlier. How much harder it must have been for a child who so desperately wanted his father's love and approval.

On Valentine's Day, Dave planned to take Marla and all the children out to dinner. Amy told me that before they left Marla's youngest daughter opened all her Valentine's gifts. Amy said it was like Christmas. She said she asked Marla's why her daughter got all the gifts. Marla replied, "Because she's special."

Amy tried to make herself invisible to Marla and Dave to avoid conflict with them. She would often sneak a phone call to me and tell me that she hated being with them. There were times when Marla took the phone away from Amy in the middle of a conversation and hung up on me. Although Amy initially resented Marla's youngest daughter she eventually made friends with her and was accepted into the circle of trust. She learned self-preservation so well that I wasn't seeing the same anger I was seeing from Evan. Maybe she saw what was being done to Evan and knew the only way to avoid being abused was to play along.

March 1999

Evan's first birthday after we moved was his thirteenth; a milestone for any child. All he wanted was a party at the Gym, like he'd had once before, and like Amy and all of Marla's children had every single year for their birthdays. Once again, Dave said that "he didn't deserve it because his grades and behavior didn't warrant it." I offered to have a party for him at the Youth Center in town, suggesting to Evan that he invite all his friends. He didn't want that. His heart was set on a party at the Gym and he held out hope that his Dad would change his mind. He didn't.

I finally arranged for a small celebration at our house. I even invited Dave. I kept thinking that my kindnesses to him would eventually pay off, wanting so badly for things to be better for Evan and Amy.

Dave did stop by. He dropped off a gym bag he'd taken from the gym's Pro shop, along with a birthday card with $10 in it. In Evan's birthday card he wrote, "I hope you get everything you want, or at least everything you deserve. Ha ha."

The ten dollars would have been fine if it had been the standard for gifts Dave gave the children. However, he spent hundreds of dollars on Marla's children for their birthdays, going with Marla to hand pick from their wish lists and taking them out to dinner. Amy didn't get as much as Marla's children did, but there were usually some gifts, along with the rubber checks.

Evan chose to hang on to the belief that more was coming. He convinced himself that when he went to Dave's on the following weekend his father's real birthday surprise would come.

Over the next weekend Evan was driven to the house by Dave to pick something up from his room. He ran in looking extremely sad. I asked him if he was okay and he said, "No one has mentioned my birthday, except one of the employees at the club who said, "Happy Birthday Evan."

Evan saw the anger in my face and panicked. I knew he didn't want me to say anything to his father but when he went upstairs to get whatever it was he needed I ran out to the driveway and asked Dave if he had any idea how much he hurt his son. Dave screamed at me to mind my own business. I saw his jaw set and the steely dark look in his eyes and I knew immediately that I'd messed up. Now Evan would pay. It took me awhile to have it sink in how awful it was for the kids if Dave found out that they relayed any information to me about what he did.

Amy later told me that Dave, Marla and the kids all went out to eat that night. Amy said she and one of Marla's daughters had felt so bad for Evan that they'd asked the entertainer to sing "Happy Birthday." Dave and Marla wouldn't let them stay to hear it.

I'd wanted Evan's birthday to be so special. For four years he had been dreaming of having a musical mixer. Dave kept promising to get him one but never delivered. Mixers are expensive. I knew I couldn't afford one on my own so I enlisted my parents, cousin and Elizabeth to all go in with me on a consolidated gift. The money was given to Elizabeth to put it into an account until Evan could find the mixer he wanted. Somehow, Dave manipulated the money from her, claiming he would put it into an account he supposedly already had for Evan so there would be even more money for the mixer.

Evan never got the mixer or saw the money.

Donna Buiso

Chapter 9

MORE AND WORSE OF THE SAME

Evan hardly saw his father after his birthday. He spent much of his time with his two best friends, Billy and Jacob, who both lived in the neighborhood. Dave's bi-monthly visitation took on a new format where Evan would do the same things on his father's weekends as he did on mine; hang out with his buddies. Often, he wouldn't even see his father the whole weekend. He would go to Billy's or Jacob's place right from my home, but was instructed not to have any contact with me during Dave's time.

Billy's mom and I gave the boys rules. They could not be down at the plaza in back of our house after 9 pm and they had to check in if they went to someone's house. Sometimes I'd see Evan down at the plaza late at night or Billy's mother would call me and tell me she didn't know where the boys were, or a neighbor would call to tell me that Evan was riding around on his bicycle after nine o'clock. If I tried to involve myself during "Dad's weekend" I was told by Evan that Dad told him not to answer to me, or to tell me that "Dad says I'm on his time now." This made it very hard for me to have any leverage as a parent. Dave undermined every decision or rule I made. I can only imagine the confusion it must have caused Evan and Amy to be caught in the middle of this.

By the fall Evan was getting increasingly out of control and was showing all the signs of being an abused child. He harbored a lot of anger which was usually directed at me. He often said the same things to me that his father said, like calling me a 'psycho'. He'd also accuse me of not being able to make a decent living. It was as though someone had tape-recorded Dave and put the tape into my son. As much as it hurt, I knew where it was coming from and I had a gut feeling that he may be using drugs. I became desperate to help my child.

One memorable weekend, Evan snuck out of the house after midnight. Once I realized he was gone, I remembered that he'd gotten a phone call earlier that night so I found the number on the caller ID and called it. The mother who answered explained that her daughter had also snuck out. We both went out to look for the kids but couldn't find them. We called the police. They told us this was very common for kids their age to sneak out in the summer and added that if they didn't show up soon we should call them back.

Common or not, I was beside myself with worry. I called a friend of mine who lived in the neighboring town whose son had hung with Evan the night before. I hated to bother him but I hoped he would have some information. He didn't. However, he felt so bad for me that he came over to keep me company and offer support. By 3:30 am I didn't want to leave any stone unturned. I knew what Evan's state of mind had been lately and my imagination went wild. I made the huge mistake of calling his father.

Marla answered the phone. She was clearly irritated that I'd woke her up. Dave got on the phone and before I could begin he bellowed, "What are you overreacting to this time?" I told him that Evan had snuck out and I had no idea where he was, or if he was okay. I just wanted to know if Dave had talked to him or had any clues as to where he might be. He yelled, "No, and don't call me again unless he doesn't come back tomorrow!!"

At 4 am I called the police back. They said they'd come over to do a report and asked me to get a picture of Evan ready. I was shaking all over as I fumbled through my things for a current photograph. At 4:30 am Evan strolled into the yard with his guitar slung over his shoulder. I felt like grabbing him and hugging the stuffing out of him, but was angry for the panic he'd caused me. He looked surprised at all the commotion and explained that he'd met up with his friend Candy at a wooded area near her house to play her some music.

After everything settled down, Candy's mother and I decided that the two would not be able to hang out again or talk to each other for at least two weeks. Evan and I talked about it. He became aware of the pain and worry this had caused me and he truly appeared to feel bad about it. He apologized and I felt fairly confident that he probably wouldn't do it again.

Dave did call the next day to see if Evan was home.

"Yes," I told him. "Candy's mother and I have reprimanded the children and they will not be able to have contact for a couple of weeks."

"Fine!" was all he said and hung up.

Evan was the model of good behavior for the rest of the week as he tried to make up for what had happened. He bubbled enthusiastically about the concert that Dave, Marla and all the children were going to at the Music Tent the following Sunday night. The performer was one of Evan's favorites and he couldn't wait to see her. There wasn't a day that went by that he didn't mention how excited he was.

On Friday, when Dave came to pick up the kids I confirmed with him about the concert as it would mean the difference between them coming home early on Sunday or very late that night. Dave assured me that the concert was still on and that they were all planning on going.

I came home Sunday after working a long shift, kicked off my shoes and collapsed in my chair. As I closed my tired eyes I wondered how the children were enjoying the concert. After a brief respite, I got up to fix myself something to eat but noticed the blinking light on my phone, indicating that I had a message. I checked it and heard the basement sounding voice Evan had when he was as low as he could get. He told me he was at Elizabeth's and asked me to pick him up when I got home from work. Confused, I called him back.

"Evan, why are you at Elizabeth's? What in the world happened? Are you okay?" I bombarded him with questions.

"Dad said I shouldn't be rewarded by going to the concert after my bad behavior last weekend. He's mad that I caused you to wake him and Marla up in the middle of the night. He demanded an apology and I just couldn't give it to him."

I told Evan that I would be right over. I was furious. Dave had led both me and Evan to believe he was going to the concert. He dropped the bomb on Evan just before they all left for their night out and then left Evan at Elizabeth's! I tried to calm the anger burning in my belly as I sped to Elizabeth's house.

I arrived and noticed that Carl was acting very cold towards me and ignoring me when I made small talk. I asked him if something was wrong. "No," he replied, "but I am mad at Evan." He wouldn't elaborate but turned on his heels to walk away from me. I was more confused than ever but my priority at that moment was my son. Evan sulked as he got in the car. He didn't want to talk about it. Once again, I told him how sorry I was but I felt unable to help him feel better.

A few days later, Amy went to visit Elizabeth. Before I could pick her up I had to first pick Evan up at his friend's house. He got in the car with me and immediately started to verbally abuse me. Evan was so nasty and out of control that I started shaking. We arrived at Elizabeth's and went inside. Evan and Amy asked if they could go in the back room to use Elizabeth's computer. I told them they could go in for a few minutes but that we had to get home. I was still disturbed over Carl's reaction to me a few days earlier and wasn't anxious to hang around, although I did want to spend a couple of minutes with Elizabeth. We had always been so close and had confided everything in each other.

I sat down with Elizabeth and Carl and started to tell them how worried I was about Evan. I expected Elizabeth to be her usual supportive self. She avoided my gaze as Carl flashed me that look that I had come to know so well. He started to question me about my responsibility in all of this. I looked at him and knew right away what was happening. I exclaimed, "Oh my God. You've been listening to Dave!" My son-in-law, like my brother, had always despised Dave but I could tell that "The Big Shift" had come.

Carl became extremely angry and started yelling at me. "Dave is a loving father. You just hate him because you think he cheated on you. You can't separate your anger at him from his goodness as a father."

It was the same diatribe that my brother had bombarded me with. I was in shock, unable to believe this was happening again. One conversation with my son-in-law was all it took for Dave. The same vile and baseless accusations were flying at me all because I was expressing concern for Evan. I hadn't even mentioned Dave.

I stood up and shouted, "Carl. The man stole $100,000.00 from your wife. How can you defend him?"

He yelled back, "Dave didn't steal that money. You gave it to him!!!" He then told me to get out of 'his' house.

Elizabeth sat there quietly, not saying a word.

I called the kids and got out of the house as quickly as I could. I thought I was going to throw up in the driveway and I cried all the way home.

The kids knew Carl had been yelling at me because they'd heard him from the back room. Evan kept asking me what Carl had said to me but I wouldn't tell him. We got home and I went straight to the kitchen as I tried to focus on the dishes I had left unwashed in the sink. I was aimlessly wiping down the counter when Evan came up behind me, put his arms around me and laid his head on my shoulder. I turned around and hugged him but no more words passed between us that night.

Just as with my brother, my relationship with my beautiful daughter deteriorated. Dave had won over my son-in-law and with him, my daughter. She started to parrot the same things to me that Carl and my brother had. It felt like a nightmare. Every support system I had was being hacked off at the knees. Elizabeth was my daughter, my best friend and my soul mate all rolled into one. I thought of all the wonderful years we had spent together before this crazy making began. Surely I was in a bad dream that I desperately needed to wake up from.

Donna Buiso

Chapter 10

TRYING TO STAY ABOVE WATER

I learned to draw from any resources I could during these hard, chaotic times. I had weekly counseling for myself and the children, I went to church, read everything I could get my hands on about child-rearing, and would talk to anyone whom I thought might be in a position to help or guide me. I even enrolled in a spiritual program called "A Course In Miracles", run by a local psychotherapist, Linda Palmer. My issues often came up during our meetings and she, like my earlier therapist, Cindy, was moved to write a letter to "whom it may concern" in the event that Dave's custody threats ever came to fruition. She and the others in the group all became extremely concerned for my children's well-being.

Amy always was an excellent student so it was hard for me to go to the school counselors and convince them of the abuse in her life. Even with Evan, I was always reluctant to approach someone unless I felt they would 'get it'. It seemed to me that almost anyone who had contact with Dave was eventually swayed, despite any training they may have had in child abuse issues.

An acquaintance of mine suggested I contact a counselor named Mike Gardinia, who ran men's groups. My friend had been in one of the men's groups and was impressed by him. I met with Mr. Gardinia as soon as I could get an appointment and, although he was friendly, I got an uneasy feeling about him. He didn't want to hear about the abuse. He just wanted to talk about being a member of Dave's gym and playing racquetball with him. That should have been my cue to not return. However, he seemed like a nice guy and my friend thought highly of him so we tried him one more time. It was just more of the same. It was blatantly clear that any attempt to get fair and helpful counseling was futile.

I decided to call Independence House and asked them for therapist referrals. They connected me to a great counseling agency who matched everyone in the family with a counselor who would be best for them. Finally I had some guidance I could work with.

One of our first meetings was with Harold, the counselor who would work with Evan. He requested a 'family' meeting and asked me to inform Dave. Of course Dave insisted on being there and I was glad he did. Dave quickly tried to take over the meeting and berated Evan in front of the counselor. "Did you bother to comb your hair before you came in here?" he snapped. "Sit up in the chair and don't even think about biting your nails." Then he berated me. "She doesn't know how to handle the kids. She's weak and ineffective as a mother. She.... She....She..." he droned on.

Harold calmly asked the children to leave the room. Once they were in their rooms and it was just the three of us, he explained to Dave how counseling works. He asked him to be more respectful of me and of his son and to allow us to be ourselves. Harold warned Dave that if he couldn't control himself, the counseling would be a waste of time.

Dave looked as though he had been slugged. He literally inched back in his chair as his face turned beet red and I saw the vein in his neck bulge. He refused to open his mouth again and just sat and glared for the rest of the session. It was one of my few moments of validation with him. However, from that time on, he hated Harold and went out of his way to discredit him to the children and to anyone who would listen.

Before the next meeting with Harold there was an incident with Evan. He and his friends went bowling and someone noticed that Evan had a few beers in his backpack. I assumed he'd taken them from his father's house because he'd just been there and I never kept alcohol in my home.

At first I wasn't informed about this. It wasn't until I learned that Evan couldn't hang out with his best friend, Billy, that I called Billy's mother to ask why. Evan and Billy were normally attached at the hip. Evan was devastated by the loss of his friend. Billy's mother explained to me, "I have alcoholism in my family. I don't want Billy anywhere near it. I'm sorry but I have to stand firm on this. Alcohol scares me. I don't feel comfortable with Billy being around Evan if there is a chance of alcohol being anywhere near my son." I explained to her that I had no knowledge of Evan ever doing this before and I promised to keep a watchful eye, but she wouldn't relent.

I called Harold. He said that as it was likely Evan did get the beer from his father's house and his father needed to be informed. I explained that this could open Evan up for even more abuse. Harold said we'd deal with that if any abuse occurred but he was adamant that his father be informed. We arranged a meeting at my home between the four of us.

Before Dave arrived, Harold and I sat with Evan and explained to him what was going on. Evan panicked and literally begged us not to tell his father about the beer. I had a sick feeling that we needed to listen to him but I had been impotent in controlling the chaos around me and felt I needed to defer to the professional who insisted it must be done. I don't think at this point that Harold realized how abusive Dave could be.

Dave pulled up in his car and Evan ran out in a panic to meet him. He grabbed Dave's cell phone and as Dave was walking into the house Evan called me from the cell phone, "Please, Mom, don't tell him. Please. Please. Please!" he begged. He was crying. I felt so torn but there was no going back at this point.

Harold told Dave what had happened. Dave sat absolutely emotionless. He had no response whatsoever. After the meeting, before Harold was even out of the driveway, Dave started to scream at Evan until his face looked like it was going to explode. "Do you know how this makes me look?" he yelled. "Do you?!"

Dave demanded that Evan leave with him. I tried to stop him but Evan hung his head as he obediently shuffled towards the door. I kept telling him that he didn't have to go, almost pleading with him. He just looked at me with his eyes full of pain. "Thanks Mom," he uttered sarcastically as he walked past me. I'm sure he felt betrayed by me and seemed resigned to go and take his punishment.

I was beside myself with worry for the rest of the afternoon. My stomach churned and my imagination tortured me with the abuse that I imagined was going on.

I was finally able to pick Evan up at the gym later in the day. He got into the car with eyes swollen from crying. He wouldn't tell me what went on but he was very angry with me. My son felt that I'd betrayed him and once again I felt sick and helpless.

I met with Harold and told him about my concerns with the stolen beers and how Evan's anger was unbearable. The verbal abuse Evan directed toward me was escalating. It seemed as though Evan couldn't help himself. After screaming insults at me then defiantly leaving the house he would come home an hour later to put his arms around me and cry, "I'm sorry Mom. Once I'm old enough to beat up Dad I know I won't do this anymore." I would hug him and tell him I understood, but I'd add that he could not continue to treat me this way. Although he'd agree, it would only be a matter of time before he'd go into another tirade.

Evan's nastiness toward Amy was also escalating. He loved to insult and demean her. Harold recommended taking out a CHINS (Child In Need of Services) on Evan, for everyone's sake. Although my heart was not behind it I knew something had to be done. I also hoped that having a probation officer working directly with Evan would help him to stay on track.

Between the CHINS, counseling with Harold, and seeing very little of Dave, Evan quickly started to get better. The verbal abuse had all but stopped and things were improving in school. I allowed myself to feel hopeful, yet again.

As Evan's fourteenth birthday approached in March, I decided to try and get him the music mixer he'd wanted for so long. Just like before, I enlisted family members and came up with the money needed for the gift. This time, however, I found out exactly what Evan wanted and bought it myself to prevent Dave from attempting to sabotage the plan.

After learning about my gift, Dave had to upstage me. He told Evan he would take him to a Crosby, Stills and Nash concert. This band was Evan's favorite at the time. Dave never did one-on-one things with Evan which made this a double gift. After the concert, I expected Evan to be brimming with tales of seeing his favorite group. However, he didn't seem excited about the concert at all and had nothing to tell me about it. His silence scared me. This was supposed to be a highlight of his life and yet he showed no sign of having enjoyed himself. It wasn't long before the ugliness between him and Dave resurfaced.

The following June, in addition to Evan working at the gym, Dave enlisted him to also mow lawns for different business associates of his with the promise of a decent wage. Evan was eager to make his own money, especially when Dave told him that he would be getting $50 to mow just one lawn. Evan ended up mowing huge lawns which took him hours. He never got paid.

I always felt that the kids were being exploited by Dave but because they didn't complain all that much I went into 'pick your battles' mode. That is until the day I noticed a man in the neighborhood staring at Amy and her friend at the bus stop. I drove to the police station and got a report of convicted pedophiles within a mile radius of our home. My heart stopped when I recognized the first face on the list as a man who was working the front desk at the gym. Dave also had him doing landscaping with Evan. I called Dave and told him what I'd found out. Although I should have been used to these reactions, it shocked me to hear him yell, "You're overreacting, as usual. Don't worry about it. I know the whole story. The guy got a bum rap. Don't bother me about this again."

I screamed into the phone, "Are you serious????"

His reply was to shut down on me. It turns out that the man's mother was a long time member at the gym and Dave had his priorities.

By the end of June, Evan confronted his father about getting paid for some of his mowing jobs so that he could buy me a birthday gift. He hadn't received any money to date, and although Dave kept saying he would get it eventually, it was clearly not coming. This caused a big argument between them after which Dave told Evan that he didn't want to see him for a while. Evan said that it was fine with him. To be sure Evan understood his wishes, Dave put in writing that he didn't care to see his son.

EXHIBIT F: Dave's letter to Evan

Evan,

I want to make sure you understand what I said to you at Elizabeth's the other day. It's clear to me that you do not want to spend time with me. I'm sorry to see that. You don' have to see me other than the time you're required to be with me and we can keep that at a minimum. I won't ask to have you with me for the next couple of weeks. Maybe that would be a good opportunity for you to think about our relationship. In the meantime I won't bother you and I will expect the same from you. I wish we could spend more time together doing things but I guess that's not to be right now. I do have to tell you that I'm disappointed in you right now. I believe you know what I mean and even you know you're a better person than you're acting at this time. At least I hope so.

Dad

The couple of weeks turned into several weeks of no communication between them. Dave never called to see Evan and Evan made it clear he didn't want to see Dave.

Chapter 11

THINGS START TO SNOWBALL

August

A few weeks after Evan received the letter from his father, a sheriff appeared at my front door and handed me a Contempt Complaint. I began to open it as Evan and Amy ran to either side of me, curious as to why a sheriff had come to the door. Evidently, Dave had filed the complaint for not sending the children for their two week visitation with him and also for getting them into counseling with counselors that he hadn't approved. He claimed to the court that we had a court order stating that we'd to agree on certain counselors. No such order existed. My stomach knotted as I realized that this was going to cost me yet another day's work. Dave was rarely sending child support and now I was being summoned to court on frivolous accusations.

A few weeks later we were in Probate Court. We sat with a court officer who looked through our file and said she couldn't find the order Dave was talking about that referred to the counseling. My lawyer stated that it was because there was no such court order. Also, I had specific days documented for Amy's summer visitation with him and I had the letter from Dave stating that he did not want to see Evan.

Instead of getting mad at Dave for wasting the court's time, the court officer turned her gaze on me. I was stunned when she asked me, "Who watches your children while you work?"

I explained that I was a home editor for a local company so I was home with my children every day except for Tuesdays, when I worked in a restaurant. I added that the children didn't get out of school until 3:30 pm and I was home by 5 pm so they were only home alone for a little more than an hour, one day a week. The restaurant was less than 10 minutes from the house and the kids always called me the minute they walked in the door.

My explanations didn't prevent her from scolding me for leaving my 'at risk' children home alone. My children were now fourteen and twelve. As we left the room, I looked at my lawyer and incredulously asked him if I'd heard right. "Really? I'm the one being reprimanded?" The lawyer just shrugged as if to say, "I don't get it either."

As Dave felt his control of Evan slipping away he worked harder and harder on Amy. His tool to gain control of Amy was Elizabeth. Although I could have never imagined it, I was now an outcast in Elizabeth's life. She was due to have her first baby, my grandchild, in July. This should have been a sacred time between us. I thought of her constantly and couldn't wrap my head around what was happening to us.

Elizabeth's friends had a baby shower for her and they invited me. I did attend but Elizabeth was very cool to me. As I was leaving she politely thanked me for coming, as if I was a neighbor. It was so painful. I had desperately wanted to share this exciting time. Instead, I was barely acknowledged and felt like a person that no one wanted to be around.

At one point during Elizabeth's pregnancy, I came home to find a horrible message on my answering machine from Dave. I heard his condescending voice reproaching me, "Elizabeth's in the hospital. I hope this makes you suffer because of the horrible mother you are. You don't deserve to have children."

There was more, but it all became a blur as I frantically started making phone calls. I called Elizabeth's house and when no one answered I left a message. I later found out that Carl was home but didn't pick up or bother to call me back. I then called the hospital and got through to Elizabeth. She told me that everything was fine and that she was going to be released within the hour. I cried and told her I loved her and how scared I was when I heard that she was in the hospital. I never mentioned Dave's call until months later when Dave and Elizabeth told the court that when she was pregnant and in the hospital, I didn't even bother to go see her.

Elizabeth went into labor almost two weeks after her due date. Elizabeth and Carl left for the hospital, leaving Amy to stay with their dog. I brought Amy some lunch, kissed her and told her that as soon as we knew anything, we'd go to the hospital together. She was happy to be helping and excitedly hugged me. "See you soon Auntie! Can't wait!" I yelled to her as I walked to the car.

In the meantime, I called Elizabeth's biological father, Ron, who lived a few towns away. He was also anxious. No one called to tell us anything so we tried to get information from the hospital. Somehow Ron was able to learn that Elizabeth was having a C-section the following morning. I called Elizabeth's house to update Amy but when she didn't answer I got a sick feeling that Dave would not let this opportunity go by without causing some kind of heartache. I called his cell phone. Marla answered and snapped at me, "We're out to dinner. Amy is fine. Don't call us again."

I called back relentlessly. Dave was not scheduled to have Amy. She was supposed to be staying at Elizabeth's dog sitting until Carl got home. Dave finally answered his phone and told me that Amy was babysitting for his cousin. I asked where that was and said I needed the number to talk to her. He replied that it was none of my business and hung up.

I called the police. They said they couldn't do much without the court order stating specific times of visitation and all our court order stated was every other weekend. They would, however, go to his house and strongly advise him to return Amy. I told them that I didn't think he was home and I didn't have the slightest idea where they might be. They replied that in that case their hands were tied.

Dave refused to answer his cell phone after he had hung up on me and no one answered at Elizabeth's home. I called the police again and asked them to go to Elizabeth's house, but no one was there. Finally, after midnight, a police officer called me back and told me that Dave's car was there but it would probably frighten Amy if they went in at that time of night. The officer, who seemed kind and sympathetic, asked me to agree to have a police officer go to Elizabeth's house first thing in the morning. He said someone could go over as early as 6 am.

By 7 am the next morning I'd heard nothing from the police. I called the station only to find out that the officer I'd talked to had gone off duty. The new officer I spoke to said he knew nothing about the situation. I explained why it was so important that I have my daughter with me on this special day. He replied, "I realize that you are having a problem with Dave. Sorry, but I'm not going to be able to help you with his. You'll have to work it out with him." He was obviously on a first name basis with Dave.

This was a complete turnabout from the previous officer. I was angry and let him know that I was the custodial parent and that Amy was supposed to be home with me. I asked for his name. He refused to give it to me but he snapped back that he would go "talk with Dave" then call me back. A short while later the officer did call me back. He informed me that Dave said to tell me that Amy would be returned to me later that day, AFTER they'd been to the hospital to see the baby.

I couldn't believe this was happening. This was about memories, milestones and sacred experiences. I so badly wanted to share meeting my grandchild with all of my children but what should have been a joyful experience was turned into a heartache.

Evan and I went to visit Elizabeth at the hospital with Ron and his other three children. It was both exciting and bittersweet. Laying my eyes on my beautiful new grandson was overwhelming, especially when I got to hold him in my arms. Elizabeth looked exhausted and I knew her labor had been difficult. I couldn't help but think about how I'd always imagined it would be when she had her first child. I had thought I'd be there for her, as she had been for me. Instead, I felt more like the great aunt who'd stopped by rather than the mother and grandmother. I wanted to cry and scream for joy at the same time.

Amy was conspicuously absent, which was something that soon became the hideous and excruciating norm. Dave waited for me and Ron's family to leave before taking Amy to visit Elizabeth, then he brought Amy home later that night. I eventually saw photographs of Amy holding her little nephew. It broke my heart that I hadn't been there to share that precious moment with her. Amy was being pulled farther and farther from me as Evan pulled farther and farther away from his father.

In September, Harold informed me that he'd filed a 51A on Dave. Evan had confided in him that his father had given him alcohol at the Crosby Stills & Nash concert and that he and Dave had both gotten a little drunk.

Exhibit G: 51A filed on September 21, 2000
DATA ON CHILDREN

Rd. ██████████ . ████████
██████████ MA.MaleDOB: ████████
DATA ON MALE PARENT
Name: ████████ Address: ████████ MA.
tel.#Age: 40+
DATA ON FEMALE PARENT:
██████████ ████ Rd. ████████ MA.
tel. # ████
DATA ON REPORTER:
Report Date: 9/21/00 Mandatory Report
Reporter's Name: ████████ , LMHC
Reporter's Address:
████████████████

Has reporter notified caretaker of report? YES: ████████
What is the nature etc.

████████ reported to me today that his father supplied him with alcoholic beverages during a concert that they attended in the recent past. He stated that it made him drunk. He further stated at this time that his father is an alcoholic and when he drinks he becomes mean to him. In the past this has caused the father to grab the boy by both wrists and force him down on his back on a couch and he then proceeds to place his face close to his son's face and threaten him.

What are the circumstances etc.

I was in the ████████ District Court at a CHINS petition hearing in which Mr. ████ made inaccurate claims about his son's non-compliance with his CHINS petition. It was an example of a long term "problem" that Mr. ████ has with his son and ex-wife in which he causes chaos in their lives by his actions.

What action has been taken thus far to treat, shelter, or otherwise assist the child(ren) to deal with this situation?

I told ████████ the seriousness of his father's actions. I have also stressed to him then as in the past the serious consequences of any and all alcohol or any drug use (as well as cigarettes) due to his age and the history of alcohol and other drug abuse on both sides of his family. In the past year and one half I have allowed ████████████ to see his father as a man with his share of problems and behaviors that have caused problems for all family members.

I have counseled him that he does not have to condone nor condemn his father for the problems that he creates and that he can choose to learn from this experience and treat his children differently if he feels that his father's style causes him or his sister and mother problems. He seems to grasp this (and most) concepts quite well. All attempts to engage Mr. ████████ in a therapeutic process have failed. He will not participate but instead attempts to sabotage the existing process.

Please give other information etc.

Mr. █████ is best described in a memo I will attach that was written by ████████ LICSW.

I would also suspect that his daughter must be affected in inappropriate ways as he "splits" her loyalties between himself and her mother who has custodial care. I would urge the Department to check with her mother and therapist to see if they feel that any action is appropriate. The Department should also be aware that Mr. ████████ allowed his current girlfriend to make a video of this female child while naked and showed it to others, including her brother ██████, likely causing a trauma to this child. Both ██████████ and ██████████ have mentioned this incident. The same woman's son who is older than ██████████ showed ████████ some very explicit pornographic videos causing considerable problems for ████████ and his mother as he acted out as a direct result of such stimulation. I would obviously question the safety of either child in that house as they are not

████████████, LMHC

safe or protected there. One would think that in the future it might be wise to supervise all visits between Mr. ████████ and his children.

EXHIBIT H: DSS's Response to Harold's 51A, September 26, 2000

The Commonwealth Of Massachusetts
Executive Office Of Health And Human Services
Department Of Social Services

ARGEOPAUL CELLUCCI
Governor

JANE SWIFT
Lieutenant Governor

WILLIAM D. OLEARY
Secretary

JEFFREY A LOCKE
Commissioner

09/26/00

Dear ▓▓▓▓▓▓▓▓,

The Massachusetts Department of Social Services has received a report that your children may have been abused and/or neglected. The report says:

Child Name	Allegation	Perpetrator
▓▓▓▓▓▓▓▓	Neglect	Biological Father
▓▓▓▓▓▓▓▓	Neglect	Father's Partner - Out of Home
▓▓▓▓▓▓▓▓	Neglect	Biological Father
▓▓▓▓▓▓▓▓	Neglect	Father's Partner - Out of Home

When the Department of Social Services gets this kind of report we are required to visit your home, see your children and talk with you and other members of your family about this report. We may also contact other people who know you and your family.

I will come to your home on 9/28/00 to meet with you.

A booklet is attached which will help explain the process. Please read it carefully. If you have any questions, please call me.

Sincerely,

Attachment: Parent's Booklet

The DSS worker conducted thorough interviews with me, the counselors and the children and summed Dave up as a 'classic abuser'. They suspected Dave was neglectful of his children and he was furious. I told Harold that I was scared. I could only imagine what Dave would do now. Harold suggested that I get a restraining order against Dave.

I went to the court house within the next couple of days and asked for a restraining order because I was afraid of my ex-husband. Judge Terrible, the other of the two judges in this Probate Court, looked at me contemptuously but granted me a temporary R.O. for one week. He told me that it was only good until the end of the week because he said he didn't want to deprive Dave of his weekend visitation with the children.

On Friday, October 6, I found myself once again facing Judge Hatchet as I tried to get the restraining order extended. He wouldn't even let me talk. I tried to speak but he just repeated the same question to me, "Has he physically threatened you within the last year?" I couldn't answer truthfully that he had, therefore the judge denied me. My last words to the judge were, "Your honor, he is going to do something drastic."

Monday was Columbus Day so the next working day of the court was Tuesday. This was my work day at the restaurant so Amy was scheduled to go to Elizabeth's after school. She would normally call me when she arrived but I never heard from her. I called and called. Elizabeth didn't answer her phone. I was beginning to panic and explained to my fellow workers that I needed to leave early.

I stopped by my house first. It was on the way to Elizabeth's and I was hopeful that maybe Amy was there. Upon entering the living room I immediately saw the blinking light on the answering machine. My heart was racing as I listened to Dave's sinister voice, "I have Amy. The letter on your bedroom dresser will inform you."

I ran into my bedroom and sure enough, there was a legal ex-parte notice giving Dave full custody of Amy until a hearing at the court in two weeks. There was no explanation about why Amy was removed from my care. Dave had, as I'd feared, taken drastic measures to punish me for the restraining order and the 51A that had been filed against him.

I became hysterical. I felt like my insides had been pulled outside my body. It was only later that I was able to wrap my head around the idea of Dave sending Amy into my room to leave the note, or, him putting it there himself.

I shook as I called one of the social workers from DSS. She was dumbfounded but said she would look into it and get back to me as soon as she could find out anything. The next morning the DSS worker let me know that Dave had told the court that Evan had threatened Amy with a knife and that I'd refused to protect her. I had no idea what he was talking about. Confusion was swirling in my head and my chest was constricting. I felt like the world was caving in on me. I was sobbing and near incoherent as I called a friend of mine who rushed to my home to calm me down.

EXHIBIT I: Ex-parte motion filed on October 10, 2000

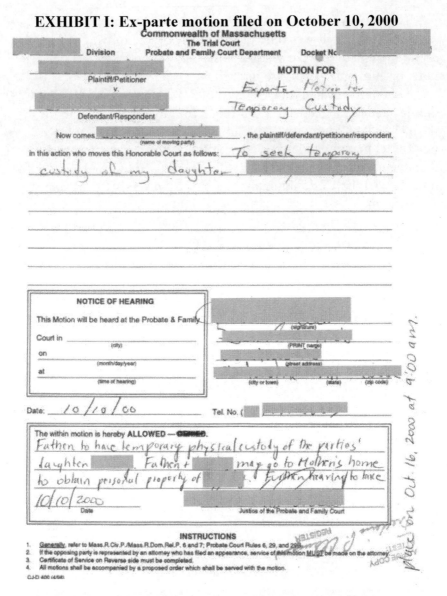

Commonwealth of Massachusetts
The Trial Court
Probate and Family Court Department

MOTION FOR Exparte Motion for Temporary Custody

Now comes ▮▮▮▮▮▮▮▮▮▮, the plaintiff/defendant/petitioner/respondent, in this action who moves this Honorable Court as follows: To seek temporary custody of my daughter ▮▮▮▮▮▮

NOTICE OF HEARING

This Motion will be heard at the Probate & Family Court in _____

Date: 10/10/00   Tel. No. (

The within motion is hereby ALLOWED — ~~DENIED~~.
Father to have temporary physical custody of the parties' daughter ▮▮▮▮. Father & ▮▮▮▮ may go to Mother's home to obtain personal property of ▮▮▮▮. Further hearing to take
10/10/2000

The 51A against Dave was thoroughly investigated and ultimately supported by the Department of Social Services. Although there was no restraining order against me, Dave, Elizabeth and her husband wouldn't let me near Amy. I wasn't even allowed to talk to her, even though she had sent me e-mails telling me that she missed me and it was Evan that was the problem; not me.

EXHIBIT J: DSS Supports 51A complaint on October 16, 2000:

The Commonwealth Of Massachusetts
Executive Office Of Health And Human Services
Department Of Social Services

ARGEO PAUL CELLUCCI
Governor
•
JANE SWIFT
Lieutenant Governor
•
WILLIAM D. O'LEARY
Secretary
•
JEFFREY A. LOCKE
Commissioner

Copy for your record

10/16/2000

Dear Ms. And Mr. ▓▓▓.

[X] As you know, I have talked with you about the recent report of suspected child abuse and/or neglect in your family which was received by the Department of Social Services. After visiting ▓▓▓ on 9/28/00, ▓▓▓ and ▓▓▓ on 10/4/00 and ▓▓▓ on 10/5/00 and talking to other people who know your family, the Department has found reasonable cause to support the following allegation(s) and the report is supported.

Child Name	• Supported Condition	Alleged Perpetrator
▓▓▓	Neglect	▓▓▓

When the Department of Social Services makes this kind of decision, we are required by law to work with you and your family to help you to change things for the better so that your children is healthy and safe.

I could barely function in the weeks that followed. It didn't help Evan to see me like that. He felt responsible for my pain even though I tried to assure him that it wasn't his fault. Friends of mine from Western Mass. drove to Oceanside to be with me. I couldn't believe that Dave had taken Amy and now I couldn't protect her from him.

I knew that Amy stayed after school on certain days, and I also knew that Elizabeth was playing mom to her as Dave wasn't about to become a full time dad. I called Elizabeth and told her that I'd be picking Amy up at school and that I felt she didn't need the responsibility of driving Amy around with a newborn at home. Besides, I missed Amy so much that I ached. Elizabeth replied "That wouldn't be a good idea." She and Dave had apparently decided that I couldn't have any contact with Amy. Even if the incident with the knife had happened the way it was being portrayed, which it didn't, supposedly Amy's fear was of her brother.

How did that warrant me being cast out of my child's life? I did not have a restraining order or any legal document keeping me from contact with Amy, yet Dave, Elizabeth and Carl all made sure that I could not get near her or even speak to her on the phone.

Weeks later, when I was finally able to see Amy, she reminded me of an incident in my kitchen that had been exaggerated by Dave to secure his motion for custody. Evan had taken one of the steak knives from the holder and made karate moves with it in front of Amy. I'd quickly grabbed the knife from him and scolded him about how someone could get hurt. There were no threats and I didn't passively let the incident go by. I could only imagine Dave interrogating Amy about what she did at home until he found something he could twist to his advantage. I'm sure he convinced her she was in mortal danger and dragged Elizabeth into the plot.

Many abusive men know the best way to hurt a woman is to hurt her children, but only an evil genius can connive a way to get one child to take the other from her mother.

Chapter 12

IN THE BEST INTERESTS OF THE CHILD?

Losing Amy devastated me.

Just a few weeks before Dave had gained temporary custody, Amy and I had gone out to Western Massachusetts to the Big E Fair. Evan hadn't wanted to go so he'd stayed at his friend's house. Amy and I had had a ball as we spent the day together at the fairground. We'd walked around with our arms locked together, went on rides and we laughed most of the day. Amy, always fearless, wanted to me to go on the Tower of Terror. I remember telling her "Amy, I love you so much I would lay down and die for you, but please don't ask me to go on that ride." Looking up at me with her big blue eyes and batting her eyelashes she'd teasingly continued to beg me as she'd hung on my arm and teased me about being a wimp. We'd walked through almost the entire fair and, although I usually restricted refined sugars, I bought Amy fudge and other treats to culminate the day. It was one of those days that will live on forever in my heart and I often wonder if she ever remembers it.

After Amy left, I opened the refrigerator and saw the fudge. I started to cry. I knew I should throw it out but I wanted it to be there for when she came home. I needed to believe that she would be back. In the meantime, I had to prepare for the upcoming court hearing.

I found a new lawyer. He was very cocky, which is why I obtained him. I felt that I needed someone strong and self-assured. The one thing that bothered me about him, however, was his preoccupation with the financial situation Dave had left me with. As unfair as it was, it was not my priority at that time. I wanted my lawyer to get me full legal as well as physical custody of both children. The counselors had suggested that it was the only way I could effectively parent them without Dave's constant undermining. I had a $2,000 tax refund that I was willing to turn over to him, along with a promise that I'd find a way to pay him anything above and beyond, as long as he was able to help me. He agreed.

On the day of the custody hearing the counselors involved with my family came to court with me hoping to testify on my behalf. Evan's counselor Harold, Amy's counselor Suzie, and the head of the counseling agency all spent the entire day in court with me because they were so concerned for my children. My lawyer happened to be out of the country and had sent a substitute lawyer in his place. I had to brief this lawyer on everything that had happened. She wasn't the least bit concerned about losing the case because of Dave's DSS involvement and the supported neglect charge. She said DSS was faxing over 18 pages of complaints against Dave and that she felt it was "an open and shut case." Dave didn't even bother to hire a lawyer. However, he did have Elizabeth and Carl with him.

While waiting for the DSS report to arrive, I had a meeting with the court officer, Alicia Pustule, my lawyer and Dave. He announced that he had a letter he wanted to read. It was from one of his employees, a woman I hardly knew. Her letter was very well written but packed full of blatant lies. She claimed to be a friend of the family who had witnessed emotional outbursts from me. She said that I'd allowed Evan to stay out all night at parties and to walk home long distances because I couldn't be bothered to pick him up. I knew the woman who wrote this letter worked for Dave under the table while collecting disability. I was furious and tried to interrupt him to explain these things wouldn't happen in a million years. It was hearsay and inflammatory and never would have been allowed in a respectable courtroom. Alicia let him read on and warned me to control my body language or I would have to leave the meeting.

We finally went before Judge Terrible who had given me the original restraining order. My lawyer argued that the incident of Evan threatening Amy with a knife never happened. The judge allowed Amy's counselor to speak. She explained that in a year and a half of counseling, Amy had never expressed fear of her brother and she had observed them interacting many times. She told the judge that in her professional opinion Amy should be immediately returned to me.

The judge then questioned Dave about the DSS report, specifically the charge of him providing Evan with alcohol. Dave called it a 'bonding experience' and stated that he felt the charge was exaggerated. The judge called a lunch recess and assured us he'd review the 18 pages of the DSS report before we resumed.

As the lunch break began, Dave disappeared only to return a half hour later with Amy. She looked scared and confused. All I could think about was the expression of 'a deer in the headlights'. On one side of the room she had her mother and her beloved counselor, and on the other side of the room was Dave with her beloved big sister. Noticing Amy's discomfort, my lawyer exclaimed that this was child abuse and said the judge would be furious about it. "Dave just sealed his coffin," she said, adding that it was all but forbidden to take children into these kinds of proceedings.

The hearing resumed and Judge Terrible didn't seem fazed by seeing Amy in the courtroom. He even allowed Amy to be interrogated by Alicia Pustule who took Amy into a private room. Alicia returned and told the judge that when she'd asked Amy how she felt about returning to her mother Amy had begun to cry. Amy claimed that if she returned to me I wouldn't let her see her father anymore, but if she stayed with her father he would let her see me as much as she wanted. My heart was breaking thinking of the lies and fear he had instilled in her. Alicia also pointed out that there was no mention of her brother, or any fear of him.

The judge, in his infinite wisdom, or bias, decided on a 'shared' custody arrangement. I would have Amy stay with me Monday, Tuesday and Wednesday and Dave would have her Thursday, Friday, Saturday and Sunday, to be returned to me Monday morning. The same judge who'd been so concerned that Dave might miss a weekend with his children had taken all of my weekends away. Three week days with school and after-school activities left me very little time with Amy. This decision completely disregarded the recommendation of the court-appointed psychologist, who had, a year earlier, declared that joint custody would not be in the best interest of the children.

EXHIBIT K: Letter from the court psychologist
COMMONWEALTH OF MASSACHUSETTS
THE TRIAL COURT
PROBATE AND FAMILY COURT DEPARTMENT
████████ DIVISION
Post Office Box ████████
████████████Massachusetts
████████, Ph.D. Court Psychologist
October 20, 1999
RE: ████████, Plaintiff
v.
████████, Defendant
Docket No.████████
STATUS MEMORANDUM
Dear Judge ████████,
I met with the minor children (████████) of the parties on 10/6/99; and with the parents on 10/20/99 as part of the services provided through the Co-Parenting Program. After a two hour meeting with the parents, it was very evident that significant differences exist as to the best interests of the minor children which will interfere with the parties developing a co-parenting plan through this office. Having reached this impasse, the parents will be relying on the court process to make a decision regarding the custodial status and parenting responsibilities" of the parties for the minor children.

████████, Ph.
 Licensed Psychologist
CC: ████████ (Pro Se)
Att. ████████(for father)

Judge Terrible also decided that we needed a 'guardian et litem' (GAL) on the case and appointed Alicia Pustule to do a two-month investigation. This gave me hope that surely an investigation would reveal everything.

The custody hearing had fallen on a Monday which meant I would be taking Amy home, at least for a few days. She had been doodling on a piece of paper as she waited at a table for the judge's decision. Her face was almost flat on the paper and she seemed afraid to look up at anyone. All I wanted to do was hold her.

After we left the courtroom Dave rushed over to me and, in front of Amy, he said, "You cannot take her until you have the legal document in your hand." We stood in tense silence while Amy lost herself in her doodling. It took less than 10 minutes for the documents to arrive but it felt like forever. I couldn't wait to leave this torturous proceeding. I looked at Elizabeth, my oldest child, whom I loved and cherished, whom I thought loved and cherished me, was crying because Amy was going home with me. Amy left with me the way she came in; head bowed and looking at no one.

After we got home I could see that Amy was in turmoil. She nervously walked around before heading into the den to zone out in front of the television. I cooked her dinner but she refused to talk to me. Dinner was ready. I asked her to come and eat with me. She said she would join me when her show was over. I waited a few minutes before I finally went into the den and turned off the TV. I asked her to come and eat before the food got cold. She began to scream at me, "Mom, what the hell??!! What is your problem?" She grabbed the phone, dialing as she rushed upstairs to her bedroom. I followed her and took the phone from her. I could hear Elizabeth asking Amy if she was okay and should she pick her up. I told Elizabeth that she needed to let Amy and me work this out and to please not make matters worse by reacting like she was doing.

Amy had thrown herself down on the floor and was still screaming at me to give her the phone. I put the phone down and sat on the floor with her. She kept screaming but I put my arms around her and hugged her as she thrashed about. She eventually calmed down and began to sob against my chest. She said that she hated her life and wanted to die. I just held her and let her cry as I stroked her hair.

We were okay for the rest of the night. However, Dave's incessant calling over the next few days would begin to put Amy back on edge with me. In spite of his attempts, I was able to distract her so that we were able to enjoy our next few days together.

Every Monday Amy would come home and be hostile toward me as she went through a hard adjustment period. She would accuse me of 'not loving or caring about Elizabeth', which had evidently become an invaluable tool for Dave. Amy loved Elizabeth, and as long as she could be convinced that I didn't, I was the enemy. No amount of refuting it helped. Elizabeth and I were estranged and that was all Dave needed to use against me. Amy was distancing herself from me. Although I tried hard to do all the things we always did, like hair brushing and watching movies, she was close but felt a million miles away. My baby had emotionally left me and the pain was all consuming.

Amy also began to severely resist counseling. She had loved her counselor. Suzie was in her twenties and would sit with Amy on the trampoline or wherever Amy was comfortable talking. Now Amy was telling me that 'counseling made things worse' and that counselors 'betray' people. She began to hide in the tree in the front yard whenever Suzie showed up for a session. It was obvious that Dave had gotten to Amy. She claimed that she didn't need to talk to anyone as long as she had Elizabeth. Amy needed counseling more than ever but Dave was never going to let that happen.

DSS remained actively involved in our case and Alicia Pustule began her investigation. When my regular lawyer returned, he asked Alicia to question certain people whom he felt were pertinent to our case. Paula had written me supportive emails that she felt should also be brought to Alicia's attention. Alicia ignored my lawyer's request and did not acknowledge Paula's emails although they were given to her.

EXHIBIT L: Paula's emails

▓▓▓▓▓aol.com wrote:

hi mom how are you ? i have most of the big
stuff out of the old place my bed and computer will be the last to go lol my
phone at the new place is messed up its busy when you cal
gotta call the phone co tomorrow lol ▓▓▓▓▓came to help move some things ,
he said he would look up ▓▓ if he could but theres over 2ooo students at
school lol still can;t believe all there is to still
do here lol were did i get all this stuff lol
                    not sure if i replied to your last email or not
of course about the car thing :}
thank you for your words of encouragement about how i raised the kids it
meant alot to me . i always wondered about the choices i made for them over
the years .you are right ididn;t have much to go by i most certainky go by
how it was for me lol but i honestly do believe if you hadn;t come into my
life things would of been so much different and none of it would been good.
                    mom i don;t know if i ever told you how you saved
me from me . you taught me how to care how to love - things like that was
never shown to me before you showed me .you showed me how thers always a
better way to look at things thank you for being such a beatiful person on
the inside as well as o the outside . thank you for loving me when noone else
did and for seeing threw
the hard ass to the real me just wanted you to know how wonderfull you
trully are . just because you hadn;t given birth to me doesn;t mean i don;t
l;ove you as much if not even more as if you had
i only had one mom and that was you .   i love you big muches xoxoxxoxo

                    love ▓▓▓

                                      09/10/00 1229

135

████████aol.com wrote:

hi mom . im sorrry about all thats
not going well with yo u , you deserve better mom , with heart as full of
love as yours only the good should enter your life .you ar right
about me not questioning you . always you see the good in people even if it
means really digging for it lol i feel bad ████ is allowing others to
influnce her ,that is not right at all unfotunatly sometimes you have to let
those you love figure it out for themselves , mom when they betray her as
well she will have learned that a mothers love will always be there
uncondiotanlly . when you will put aside your own hurt and open your heart
and arms to her she will know what i already know .
Don;t let them get to you - you know
your heart is always true . If i had to pick a perso n who changed and or
influenced my life it would have to be you . You have shown me
that there is beaty in everyone if you only look deep enough .You have shown
me love is not a weakness but i gift to be shared even if it doesnlt turn out
as one planned.you have showed me
even tho people in my life tried telling me otherwise i am a good person and
i have self worth .
you have showed me to be kind to others even when they don;t deserve it .
Mom i wish i could explain in words
how you saved me from me but believe it or not there are no words that come
close to what a trully beatiful loving person you are .

i love you mom   ████ xoxoxoxo

Many people wrote letters of support for me, but as with Paula's
e-mails, they were ignored. In the meantime, there was nothing but
anger and chaos around me and the whole situation was taking a
severe toll on Evan who began to spiral out of control.

Chapter 13

DSS – GAL - Addiction

Unlike my experience with DSS in Western Mass., the workers at the Oceanside DSS office were very knowledgeable in domestic violence and highly concerned with the welfare of my children. The first worker who investigated our case, Mia, was sympathetic and worried. It had been her job to support (or not) the 51A that was filed by Harold. She had talked to me, Harold and to Amy and I knew she 'got it' when she told me that she was concerned by Amy's body language and about what she didn't or wouldn't say. She said it suggested a domestic violence pattern and assured me that the agency would do what it could to help us. She told me that they would follow up on everything that had been reported and come up with a plan.

The next worker, Kay, was assigned to do a more thorough assessment of the family. She sat on my living room sofa with Evan and questioned him about his father. She listened to him rant about Dave's cruelty and how he'd stolen Evan's beloved guitar, as well as the money that he had acquired for his sound mixer. She promised him she'd get the guitar and the money back.

Kay told me that upon meeting with Dave she immediately recognized the abuser profile. She also said that when she visited Amy at his home, Amy was quite different there. She was always bubbly and running around my house doing gymnastics, but at Dave's house she was rigid and needed his permission to get a glass of juice.

Alicia Pustule was simultaneously running her investigation. She refused to interview the people my lawyer and I had asked her to interview, but she did interview anyone Dave requested, including Marla. Although the investigation was supposed to be wrapped up before Christmas, Alicia asked for another month to complete her report. I was very unhappy that I was going to have to continue with the "shared" custody arrangement through the holidays.

I could feel Amy slipping farther and farther away from me. On the three days that Amy stayed with me she had school, cheerleading practice and homework. I had very little time with her, and what little I did have Dave relentlessly tried to usurp. He always had something Amy needed to do: "Elizabeth needs you to babysit," or "We're going to dinner and we don't want to leave you out." If I tried to refuse she would throw tantrums and leave my house on Wednesday furious with me.

On the four days that Amy was with Dave, from Thursday through Sunday, I couldn't even talk to her. If I called the house, Dave hung up on me stating that this was 'his time' to be with her. I knew almost nothing about what she did and who she hung out with. I do know that Dave took her out of state without informing me. The children were now on State Health Insurance and since I held her health insurance card it would have seemed reasonable that he let me know in case of an emergency.

Just before Christmas, Amy had a cheerleading display with her team at the Oceanside County Mall. Dave was already there when I arrived. Amy refused to acknowledge me. I felt like a ghost on the sidelines.

My neighbor, Wendy, who also had a child in the same event, had become very friendly with Dave and stood near him. Dave had his arms folded and his steely, ice cold stare was fixed on Amy, but it was occasionally darted in my direction. He had a Christmas party to attend later that night and left Amy's event early, but not before arranging for Amy to be driven back to his house by my neighbor.

After Dave left Wendy got an emergency phone call and asked me if I could take Amy home because she had to leave immediately. Amy was horrified to hear about the change in plans. She closed up inside herself like a clam. I could feel the fear emanating from her as we got into the car and drove the short distance to my old home.

As we approached what was now Dave's house on the dark dead end street I noticed there wasn't a single light on in the house. I knew from living with Dave that he never locked his doors. Uncomfortable about leaving her alone in this dark unprotected house I suggested to Amy that I take her back to my house until Dave could pick her up.

She panicked. "No!!! No!! I can't go to your house. Drop me off now! Dad will be furious!" "Dad went to a party and who knows what time he'll be back," I told her. "He can come get you on his way home." She became hysterical.

As I drove the three streets over to my house Amy grabbed my cell phone and dialed her father. "Dad. Mom's taking me to her house. I can't help it!!!!" she screamed. She was sobbing as she walked into the house beside me. I tried to console her and said everything would be okay but she just put her hand up as if to say "I'm not listening." She paced the floor and kept looking out the window for Dave.

Within fifteen minutes a car was peeling down the road with its horn blaring. Amy ran out the door and jumped into the waiting car of her father. I just watched with that all too familiar pit in my stomach as they pealed out of the driveway.

Shortly after this incident, Dave and Marla went on a trip out of the country. Dave made arrangements for Amy to stay with the same neighbor, Wendy, without ever informing me. He knew that I would see Amy walk by my home on her way from the bus stop. When I first saw her I ran out to talk to her. I tried to insist that she come stay with me instead of the neighbor. She became so hysterical that I didn't pursue it. I couldn't bear to see her fear for just being around me if her father had told her not to be. I felt that if I just had a few good days with her, without constant harassment from Dave, that we might get back to the way things used to be between us. However, no amount of trying to reason had any effect.

I kept DSS informed of everything. They assured me that Dave's abuse would come out in the end. In response to Alicia Pustule asking for another month, Kay from DSS said, "D, won't it be worth it to finally have this reign of terror over?"

Kay explained to Alicia that the State had been picking up the tab for health insurance on the children because Dave refused to pay it, in spite of the court order requiring it. According to Kay, Alicia didn't seem to care about it.

Alicia Pustule finally completed her report. She had been made aware of the DSS report about the alcohol supplied to Evan by his father and Evan working with the registered pedophile at the Gym. She'd also received a report about Amy's broken nose, which had occurred during an accident on an unsupervised trampoline at Dave's house, and Dave's lack of concern over this resulting in her not receiving any medical attention for over 24 hours. Alicia was given copies of the other 51A's filed against Dave, including the ones in Western Mass, and the one filed by Independence House shortly after my intake. She knew that of all the DSS interviews with Amy there were never any expressions of fear regarding her brother. In fact, she told Alicia that she missed him.

EXHIBIT M: Excerpts from the GAL Report
"When asked about the present shared custody arrangement, Amy responded that it works out "okay." She said there are no problems between her and her brother and that they get along "fine.""

Alicia spoke to my friend Mary who had gone to the court and demanded to be interviewed. Mary had known me for thirty years and she assured Alicia that I was a loving, supportive mother. She'd also explained how inappropriate Dave had been with Elizabeth when she was a teenager.

Amy was now twelve and one of my big concerns involved her sleeping in her father's bed. I only discovered this after I'd asked Amy if she slept with her kitty at night, to which she'd responded, "No, I sleep in Dad's bed with him every night." Alicia put in her report that I had a problem with it; not that it was a problem.

From the GAL Report:

When this probation officer asked Amy, specifically, about sleeping arrangements with father, she responded that she sleeps at father's most of the time but also stays at Marla's and Elizabeth's as well. When asked if she sleeps in her own bedroom at father's house, Amy's tone got defensive when she replied, "I no longer sleep with my dad because you told him I couldn't."

Alicia also interviewed Marla although she only devoted a few paragraphs to her. One statement seemed to sum up Marla's attitude regarding her children versus Amy and Evan.

From the GAL Report:
"Her youngest child, XXXXX, age eleven, is Amy's best friend. XXXXX, she said, although she is younger, is a great role model for Amy because she is motivated, happy and well adjusted. She said all three of her children possess these attributes."

I'd also had a concern about Amy's Rocky Horror Picture Show Halloween costume from the year before. She'd worn an extremely short skirt with fishnet stockings and high heels and too much makeup for a child her age. Ever since the bathtub incident in Western Mass, Amy had started coming home with provocative clothing and make up. When I saw her after Halloween I would not let her wear the costume and threw it out. I didn't think to save it to show the court. I did show a photograph of Amy in her costume to Alicia but she said she "had no problem with it."

When Evan's probation officer, Bret, received a call from Alicia, the logical question for her to ask him would have been if he'd seen any violent behavior in Evan. Instead, she asked him who the better parent was. Bret chose Dave.

From the GAL Report:
"Mother, Mr. B stated, has to stop portraying herself as a victim. He does not believe Evan's situation is exacerbated by father's actions. If the court were to ask for his recommendation, he would side with father."

In spite of all Evan's testimony to the abuse he'd suffered from his father, when Bret met Dave they bonded and Bret became a member at the gym.

Alicia's interview with Elizabeth took up a page and a half of the report. My daughter, whom I'd raised alone until the age of fourteen, who'd been closer to me at one time than any human being on earth, changed history. She gave Dave all the credit for raising her. She even blamed me for not having Dave at her second wedding even though it had been her and Carl's decision not to invite him to the ceremony.

She repeated all the unfounded lies that Dave had propagated, bringing up a depression I had suffered for a brief period when she was an eight years old and most likely hadn't even remembered. This was something I had told Dave about in our early years together.

From the GAL Report:
"Elizabeth reiterated what her stepfather told this writer that she believes her mother has mental health issues. She said her mother had a nervous breakdown when Elizabeth was a young child and Elizabeth was sent to live with her maternal aunt, ████████, for a while."

I explained to Alicia that Elizabeth never went to live with her aunt, who was not really her aunt but my cousin Gina. I had suffered a horrible loss when Elizabeth was eight years old which had put me into a depression. In those days, it was not uncommon to be hospitalized for a few days while a patient's medications were stabilized. Elizabeth often spent time with my cousin Gina because Gina had a son the same age as Elizabeth and we often took turns taking the children. I couldn't imagine Elizabeth even had a memory of this and had to believe it was Gina or Dave who had supplied the information, especially as Elizabeth was only there for about five days.

I also noted that in Elizabeth's interview Alicia stated, "She said she has always had a "very" close relationship with Amy since her birth."

Although Elizabeth always loved her brother and sister dearly, Amy was five months old when Elizabeth left the house, first to spend the summer with a friend of mine to get away from Dave, then to go off to college for four years. Shortly after Elizabeth's graduation we moved out to Western Mass. Their "very" close relationship actually started when the custody became an issue.

Both Evan's and Amy's counselors were interviewed by Alicia. They'd shared with me their responses to her questions in the interview, but Alicia's report twisted everything they said. They each got three paragraphs.

I was stunned to learn that Alicia reported the exact opposite of Kay's observations of Amy in the two homes, stating that Amy was more at ease at her father's house and acted guarded with me. Even though Alicia knew that Dave had a male roommate who was in his forties she didn't think it important to interview him. The fact that the kids reported him to be weird and that Dave blamed him for the pornography films that Evan saw when he was ten didn't seem to faze Alicia or warrant her looking in to.

Alicia's recommendations at the end of her three months of interviews were that things remain the same with the custody arrangements. She said that I portrayed myself as a victim. I found this ironic as DSS had required in my plan that I attend support programs through Independence House and that I also attend extra Al-Anon meetings. She added that Dave was "possibly controlling and manipulative", also ironic because DSS had put in his plan that he go to batterer's classes designed to help men manage their anger towards women. The DSS workers were shocked, as were the counselors, when Alicia went against their recommendations. As one counselor put it, "She was more interested in pleasing the judge than looking for the truth."

I was heartbroken and totally disillusioned. I thought the GAL was going to be the truth finder. I had been assured by DSS that it would be over. It wasn't, not by a long shot.

This was not just taking a toll on me; it was taking a huge toll on Evan. He saw my pain and continued to feel responsible for it. No amount of reassuring him changed that. Between the CHINS, Harold's guidance, the Alternative Learning Program at the High School, and not having any more visitations with Dave, Evan's behavior had been getting better in spite of all this craziness.

Alicia had submitted her report in January 2001. In May of that same year, Amy was at my home for her usual three days when Dave called to talk to her, as he always did when she stayed with me. I was at work when Evan answered the phone. He took the opportunity to tell his father he wanted his guitar back. Dave apparently taunted him and egged him on to come to his house to get it. He said he'd give it to him if he dared come over.

Evan later explained that he'd sprinted the three streets over to his father's house and had found Dave waiting for him. When he saw Evan step on to his deck Dave had shut the slider doors on him. Blindsided, Evan had lost his temper and knocked Dave's planters off the deck. Dave quickly called the police. I couldn't help but feel that it was a another of Dave's set ups, reminiscent of how Dave would set me up and call the police after I reacted to something he'd instigated. Evan was arrested. He already had the CHINS on him so this incident only made matters worse. Before this happened, I had tried to drop the CHINS because Evan was doing so well. Bret had refused to drop it because Dave objected, even though I was the custodial parent. Evan had tried so hard to do better only to be sabotaged by his father.

Dave reported to Evan's P.O. that Evan was using pot. He knew this because Elizabeth had copied conversations she'd had with Evan over Instant Messenger where he had made references to pot. Elizabeth had turned them over to Dave who then turned them over to Bret. Evan, who loved and trusted Elizabeth as much as Amy did, felt bitterly betrayed.

After he got home from his meeting with Brett, Evan went straight for the phone and called Elizabeth. Although he was upstairs he was talking so loud and forcefully that I couldn't help but hear every word. "How could you do this to me? You know how mean Dad is to me, especially when he's drinking! How would you feel if Carl treated your son like Dad treats me?"

My heart broke for him as he hung up, angry and distraught. He came back downstairs and looked at me with confusion. "All she could say to me was, 'He doesn't drink to get drunk.'" I don't know how Elizabeth had responded to his questions but it seemed clear by that statement that she'd loyally defended Dave.

My pain for my children was intense. No one except me and Harold validated Evan. His paternal aunt and uncle, and even his paternal grandfather, ignored his existence because he was estranged from his father. Now his beloved sister was denying his feelings too.

Shortly after Evan's arrest, we went to Juvenile Court on the charges that were brought against him for breaking Dave's plants. His father was sitting upstairs with the Victim Witness advocate. It was so unbelievable to me that these roles were reversed - wasn't Evan the victim and Dave the aggressor? I had Evan's educational advocate with me. She had written a letter to the court documenting Evan's abuse and the symptoms that he displayed because of it.

EXHIBIT N: Letter from educational advocate 12-21-00
Your honor,

My name is ███████████, and I am ██████'s educational advocate. I have attended many meetings to assure that he gets the proper education, but what I have seen is that "proper education" means different things to many different people. The understanding of "emotional abuse" is sometimes beyond the scope of a public school system's administration, as, I'm sure you will agree it is beyond the scope of most people. When there are no visible scars, (and we are a visual society as a whole), we tend not to believe in this type of abuse.

I have been educated by the finest organizations on domestic violence/abuse. I worked for Independence House as a court advocate, and spent many years working for Safe Harbor teaching "Women's Empowerment Through Self-Defense." I am currently the director of the ███████ office of the "Federation For Children With Special Needs" as well as an educational advocate, but I also got my experience from the best teacher, life.

An emotionally abused child cannot be held accountable for how the abuse in their life has affected them. They cannot be bullied, by a system, any system. Especially when the abuse is ongoing. Juvenile court is not the answer to █████'s needs for an education. Stopping the abuse is what is needed. When the abuse is stopped, and the child gets counseling, the school performance goes up, and the child believes that someone really cares about what they're going through. No one in the ██████████ school system has honored him. They have consistently denied him the right to feel the pain and suffering that he has been subject to. Some of the characteristics of an abused child are:

1) A marked change in academic performance
2) Exhibits extremes of behavior
3) Unpleasant, hard to get along with
4) Engages in use of drugs and or alcohol
5) Extreme mood swings

All of these characteristics are present in ▮▮▮▮ profile. This is not by coincidence. What ▮▮▮▮ needs is for everyone to honor his challenge to survive the abuse. To nurture and respect him for what he has to endure on a daily basis. Give him support and guidance through counseling, both in and out of school. Tailor his academics so that he can feel success, and stop making academic demands that only exacerbate his feelings of self-worthlessness. Teen suicide and self-medication are on the rise because no one is listening to their pain.

I'm asking that ▮▮▮▮'s emotional disability and pain be validated by the court, by dropping the "CHINS" petition, and ordering that the school undergo sensitivity training for "emotional domestic violence" and how it manifests in children. I am available to them for this training at any time. The State Juvenile Justice "Guiding Principles of DYS" begins with "Holding youths accountable for their behavior", but nowhere does it ask, "When a child can't be held accountable, what do you do?" Hold the abusive person accountable. The juvenile court system is not the forum for demanding a child excel in academics. Knowing ▮▮▮▮'s I.Q. and academic abilities, he is obviously going against the adults that placed him in front of you. If he is left alone, he will be able to succeed in his own time. If he fails school, regardless of the reason, he will only be held accountable for his decisions by staying back a year. But if he gets the proper support from the adults around him, including the school, we may be able to salvage the ▮▮▮▮ that he is able to be.

Thank you for your consideration in this matter. Enclosed is a handout about emotional disabilities/abuse. Please read this before you make your determination, and you will be reading about many of the children who are brought to you for the same reason.

Thank you

▮▮▮▮▮▮▮

Her letter was waved aside by Brett who dismissed its contents with "I don't buy that crap."

That same day, Evan was tested for marijuana and failed. The court took this as proof that his father was right about everything. As usual, Dave came out smelling like a rose. Once again, I stood in amazement at how everything had gotten turned around.

Evan was now on official probation with curfews and academic standards that he was required to meet. My son became lost in his anger and he often disappeared past his curfew. I'd spend many hours looking for him and would find him drunk somewhere in the neighborhood. I discovered liquor hidden in his boots and his backpack. I also found it buried in the leaves outside our home. I'd filed a complaint against Brett which resulted in him being taken off of Evan's case. I kept DSS informed about everything and let them know what was going with Evan's new P.O. She was an attractive young woman who sympathized with Dave and blamed me for my lack of control.

In August of 2001, Evan came home from hanging out with his friends in the neighborhood and complaining that his jaw hurt. The next morning he couldn't close it. He admitted he'd gotten into a fight with one of his friends. I took him to the ER and we discovered that he had a broken jaw.

I will never forget standing over him as he came out of anesthesia after four hours of surgery. Seeing him with his jaw all wired up was heart wrenching and I remember wishing to God that I could take the pain for him. As he awoke, the first thing he said through his wired teeth was, "Don't tell Dad. I don't want him here." I explained that I had a legal responsibility to tell his father he'd been hospitalized but if he didn't want to see him that was his decision.

Dave did later come to the hospital and found Evan lying in bed with an intravenous in his arm. Evan bristled when his father walked in but he managed to say "Are you giving me my guitar back?" Dave shot back, "I'm not going to discuss that!"

"If you're not going to give me my guitar back, then leave!" Evan cried with as much emphasis as he could muster through his clenched jaws.

As I watched the scene unfold I realized that as much as Evan wanted his beloved guitar back, it had become a symbol of Dave's control by withholding not just the guitar, but also his love.

Evan winced as he closed his eyes and blinked back tears. I haven't often felt real hatred in my life, but this was definitely one of those moments. I couldn't imagine how a father could see his son like that and be so cold and cruel to him.

I tried to comfort Evan but he was embarrassed and rebuffed me. I walked over to the door, not wanting him to see the tears that were in my own eyes. From the doorway I could see Dave at the nurses' station. He was asking questions one would expect a concerned father to ask. "Is my son going to be okay? Will his jaw return to normal?" He wore a look of consternation on his face that was not there previously. The nurses began to giggle as Dave flirted with them. Within minutes he had them all laughing. I wanted to vomit. Dave left and never returned to the hospital or reached out to Evan in any way.

Because he had violated his probation order, Evan could not leave the hospital and come home with me. He had a choice; either he enter a recovery program at Gosnold, a residential rehabilitation center, or be sent to juvenile lock-up. Evan did not want to go to Gosnold.

I was so distraught thinking of my son in a lock-up, especially with his jaw wired, that I sought comfort in the rectory. The hospital Chaplain asked if she could do anything for me. She listened to my story and comforted me then promised to do whatever she could to help Evan. She was another angel sent into our lives. After she'd talked to me and Evan she apparently recognized the urgency of his predicament and made some phone calls. She also arranged for Evan to talk with someone about the treatment program and he finally agreed to go to Gosnold.

Getting Evan admitted wasn't easy. There weren't any beds available. It was only because of the intervention from the hospital Chaplain that we were successful in getting Evan admitted. I don't know how she did it, but Evan was accepted into Gosnold. I kept him supplied with pureed food and shakes because he couldn't eat the cafeteria food with his wired jaw.

After two weeks, Evan came out of rehab with his jaw still wired and still wanting to drink alcohol. If any seeds of recovery had been planted by the program it wasn't evident to me. I had doubts about whether two weeks in an adult facility could do anything for him; he clearly needed a much longer recovery period. Harold agreed. However, the real benefit was knowing where he was and having him safe and away from substances, even for that short time.

Evan's drinking only escalated after this. I pleaded with the powers that be at Juvenile Court to get him some help because he was constantly being written up for violating his probation by drinking. My son was not a criminal; he was a child with an illness that nobody wanted to treat. Dave was now suggesting that the court turn Evan over to him because I was 'ineffective' as a parent. I reached out to a social worker at Juvenile Court and told them Evan shouldn't be allowed at his Dad's house because of the abundance of alcohol and lack of supervision. "If he's an alcoholic, then he has to learn to be around alcohol without indulging," was the reply I got.

One night, not long after Evan left Gosnold, he came home from hanging around the neighborhood with some friends and went right upstairs without speaking to me. I yelled up to his bedroom that I'd kept his dinner warm. He yelled down that he didn't want it. A few minutes later, I went up to talk to him and found him passed out on his bed next to a puddle of vomit on his sheets. It seemed to me that Evan couldn't leave the house for an hour without coming home drunk or high. He had so much hurt and anger inside of him but had nowhere to put it, except on me.

Evan's male role model was his abusive father. Many times, I could close my eyes and hear my ex-husband in my son's rage. The verbal abuse intensified, and although Evan was never physically abusive to me, he was abusive to himself and to property. In a fit of anger, he punched the wall and broke his hand, sending his knuckles to his wrist. He would smash things around the house and more than once I was forced to call the police on him. I did it out of desperation as much for him as for myself. Evan began to hate me for what he felt was a betrayal, and whatever seeds Dave had sown about me were sprouting in Evan's need to blame someone for his pain.

I drove around the neighborhood looking for Evan for hours one night and I eventually found him at a party in town. He reluctantly got into my car then looked at me in a drunken haze before asking, "How could you hate your own son? How could anyone hate their own son?" I knew it wasn't me he was talking to – he was projecting his father on to me. My heartache was overwhelming. As angry as I was at him, all I wanted to do was hug him and make his pain go away.

I know I didn't always handle things perfectly. I did handle things the only way I knew how. I hope, someday, that Evan will look back and understand my concern and my fear for him and for what was going on with Amy; especially if he went into a rage on the rare occasion that she was home. I made the mistake of letting Evan know this even though I knew he already blamed himself for Amy's absence from the house. I was torn in two directions, trying to focus on both children and their needs, while trying desperately to salvage what was left of their emotional wellbeing. It was as though I was watching one child self-destruct while the other was being washed out to sea. I tried desperately to throw them both life lines.

I reported Evan's drinking to his probation officer regularly but had only the smallest of hopes that she would do anything to help him. The alternative was that I do nothing. I didn't realize, however, the extent of the possible consequences for Evan breaking the rules of his probation. Following one of my reports to the P.O. my son was be taken into custody and marched into a police holding cell for a few hours. I was horrified to see my child in wrist and ankle shackles. Once Evan was processed I was given the option to bail him out. The DSS worker had advised me against it, suggesting that it might be in Evan's best interest to give custody over to DYS (Department of Youth Services). She also told me that DYS didn't have the rehab programs that Evan was in dire need of. I had learned not to trust the system and decided to bail Evan out. He was good for a while, but it didn't last.

As Evan's drinking resumed, I was once again out looking for him in the dead of night, terrified that I might find him dead by the side of the road. Evan knew that I was going to report him to his P.O. and Dave saw this as an opportunity to reach out to Evan after a year and a half of not being in his son's life.

After Dave dropped Amy off at my home one afternoon he asked Evan to come out to the car. He then offered Evan $20 and drove him to the corner store to buy cigarettes. I'd refused to give Evan money during that time because I didn't want him buying pot or alcohol. Evan later told me that his father had waited outside of a convenience store while Evan petitioned someone to buy cigarettes for him. Evan had complained to his father that I'd turned him in to his P.O. all the time and wanted him to enter rehab.

Dave had assured our son that he would never do that. After this incident, Evan would often come and threaten me that he would go live with Dave because he could do whatever he wanted with his father. He'd snap at me, "Dad understands that it's no big deal to have a couple of beers with my friends."

Things just got worse. I tried talking to Juvenile Probation but no matter who the P.O. was, they only listened to Dave. Although Evan had reported the abuse from Dave to the psychologist from Juvenile, when he first went on the CHINS, no one would reference that particular file. One P.O. even suggested to me that Evan might be better off living with Dave. I was incredulous. I told them Dave drank a lot and had liquor all over the house, to which the P.O. again responded that if Evan were an alcoholic then he'd have to get used to being around alcohol, even if he was sober.

After much pressure from me, one of the P.O.'s finally came up with a plan to send Evan to the forestry camp for boys. It wasn't the rehabilitation I had asked for, but she assured me that "kids come back with a whole new attitude."

Evan couldn't get into the program until March. I counted the weeks. He was furious with me for pushing for this and his father fueled this anger. In front of the P.O. Dave would appear to be extremely supportive of the idea, but in front of Evan he was totally against it.

Evan went to the Forestry Camp for about four weeks, which included his sixteenth birthday. He wasn't allowed contact with anyone outside the camp and no one was allowed to visit or pick him up there. At the end of his stay I was told that I couldn't pick Evan up at the camp but to pick him up at Juvenile Court. In spite of these rules, however, when I arrived to pick Evan up I discovered that Dave had already managed to collect him from the Camp. By the time Evan saw me it was a few days later. After spending this time with Dave he was angrier than ever at me. I knew Dave blamed me when Evan screamed at me about what I had done to him.

Three weeks after his sixteenth birthday, while still on probation, Dave picked Evan up in the late afternoon to have him spend the night at his house. Just before I went to bed there was a knock on the door. It was the local police. They'd found Evan face down and beaten up at the local beach at around 10:00 pm. He had urinated on himself. The police had called an ambulance and had Evan transported to the ER. They said they'd tried to call me but my phone was busy. I had been using the dial-up connection to the Internet. They had also tried to call Dave but got his answering machine. What they didn't know was that Evan had a court-ordered 9 pm curfew.

I tried to call Dave on my way to the hospital but didn't reach him until 11 pm, just as I was rushing into the ER. Dave sounded like he'd been drinking and asked me if he should come to the hospital. I told him no and hung up.

Evan was still very drunk when I arrived. The moment he saw me he tried to get up, his arms outstretched to hug me, but his legs buckled beneath him. He was dressed in a thin T-shirt that was badly ripped from the fight he had evidently been in. He had no memory of going to the beach or of who had beaten him up. Apparently a passerby in a car had heard the commotion and called the police. It was the middle of April and still very cold at night. Had he not been found he most likely would have ended up with hypothermia.

The doctor explained to me that Evan's blood alcohol level was over 200 and that he wanted Evan to spend the night in the ER to make sure that he didn't aspirate.

Seeing my bruised son laying on a gurney, so intoxicated that all he could do was cry and tell me how sorry he was, was excruciating beyond words.

EXHIBIT O: ER Report

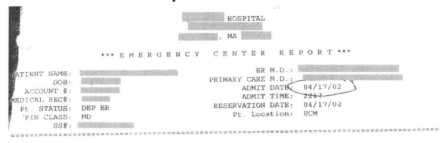

```
                              ▓▓▓▓▓   HOSPITAL
                        ▓▓▓▓▓ , MA ▓▓▓▓▓

                 *** E M E R G E N C Y   C E N T E R   R E P O R T ***

PATIENT NAME: ▓▓▓▓▓▓▓▓▓▓           ER M.D.: ▓▓▓▓▓▓▓▓▓
        DOB: ▓▓▓▓▓       PRIMARY CARE M.D.: ▓▓▓▓▓▓▓▓▓▓▓▓▓
  ACCOUNT #: ▓▓▓▓▓              ADMIT DATE: 04/17/02
MEDICAL REC#: ▓▓▓▓▓             ADMIT TIME: 2217
  Pt. STATUS: DEP ER       RESERVATION DATE: 04/17/02
  FIN CLASS: MD                Pt. Location: ECM
        SS#: ▓▓▓▓▓▓▓
```

CC: 16 year old came to the ER via rescue for alcohol intoxication.

HPI: Patient does admit to a six pack of beer tonight. Police had been involved for ? assault or injury. They called rescue to transport him to the ER for facial injuries.

SHX: Staying with his father tonight normally lives with his mother.

PMHX: None.

ALLERGIES: None.

MEDS: None.

ROS: Patient denies altercation, LOC, does admit to the alcohol. Patient not very cooperative, crying, requesting to go home. States he remembers his father's phone er but not his mother's and he lives with his mother.

PEI: Patient has slurred speech. Strong odor of alcohol. PERRLA. EOM with nystagmus literally with extreme gaze. Conjunctiva are injected no exudate. Multiple abrasions to the right shoulder, right head and does have some blood at the nares. Scalp is intact other than the abrasions. No step off or lacerations. No cervical spine tenderness. Trachea is midline. Lungs are clear. Heart sounds S1,S2 no extra heart sounds or murmurs. No subcutaneous emphysema. No crepitus to the ribs. Abdomen is soft, nontender with normoactive bowel sounds. Moving all extremities. ROM is intact all joints. Nares without septal hematoma. No active bleeding. Teeth are intact. Pharynx is pink. SA O2 is 99 percent on room air. Temp is 97.3. Pulse is 115. Respirations are 28. BP 159/86

ED COURSE: Mother was contacted. The clerks found the phone number called her and they were not able to reach the father. Mother states that she is been trying to deal with his alcoholism. He has just turned 16 at the end of March and he is already been in Gosnold for alcohol abuse and he just got out of Homeward Bound. He has had a fx jaw last summer from altercations when drunk. His abrasions were cleaned. It was advised to the mother that she go home and come back in the morning to pick him up. He spent the night in the ER. Patient was awakened in the morning he was alert and oriented remembered most events from the night. Pupils remained round and equal. Moving all extremities. GCS is 15.

Labs: Alcohol level that was over 200. RDS is negative other than the alcohol.

DISCHARGE DX: 1. Head injury.
               2. Alcohol intoxication.
               3. Multiple abrasions and contusions.

I   RUCTIONS: Patient was given head injury sheet. He was advised no alcohol. Consider

```
▓▓▓▓▓▓▓▓  *PCI LIVE* (PCI: OB Database LIVE)
Run: 05/03/02-16:37 ▓▓▓▓▓▓▓▓▓▓            Page 1 of 2
```

Dave flew into damage control. He knew this had happened on his watch so he made sure he beat me to the hospital the next morning and picked Evan up at 6 am.

Exhibit P: Police Report about the above incident

```
04/30/2002                        Police Department                    Page: 1
Ref:                      NARRATIVE FOR PTL.
        Entered: 04/29/2002 @ 1608              Entry ID: 226
        Modified: 04/30/2002 @ 1225            Modified ID: 744
        Approved: 04/29/2002 @                 Approval ID: 137
```

On 04/17/2002 at approximately 2133 hours, Sgt. ▓▓▓▓and I were dispatched to the ▓▓▓▓
Beach Parking Lot for a report of a group of intoxicated individuals causing a disturbance. Upon
arrival I observed a male juvenile laying on the ground in the far right corner of the lot. The
individual, later identified as ▓▓▓▓▓▓, was conscious but extremely intoxicated and had
urinated himself. Sgt. ▓▓▓▓ requested rescue to the scene at this time due to his extreme
state of intoxication and for the apparent minor injuries he had somehow sustained. Mr.
▓▓▓▓ had great difficulty speaking coherently and was unable to provide me with any
information except his name, age, and phone number (after numerous requests). He would
not or could not recall what had happened to him, how he got there, and denied having
consumed any alcohol.

Sgt. ▓▓▓▓ spoke with independent witnesses at the scene who reported to him that Mr.
▓▓▓▓'s injuries were a result of him falling due to his state of intoxication. **SEE SGT.
▓▓▓▓'S SUPPLEMENTAL REPORT***

▓▓▓▓Rescue arrived on scene and transported Mr. ▓▓▓▓▓▓for evaluation. ▓▓▓▓
Rescue attempted to contact Mr. ▓▓▓'s mother,▓▓▓▓, multiple times via telephone, with negative
results. I then proceeded to her residence at ▓▓▓▓▓▓Rd. and advised her in person.

Approximately 3-4 days later I spoke with Ms.▓▓▓▓via telephone regarding the incident. I informed
her at this time that her son was extremely uncooperative and would provide us with very little
information. Ms.▓▓▓▓told me she thought she knew who her son had been with, but ▓▓▓ would
not verify nor did she feel he would tell the police. I advised Ms.▓▓▓▓to speak with Sgt .▓▓▓▓
regarding the event, as he had spoken with the witnesses at the scene and would possibly have
more information.

PTL. ▓▓▓▓▓▓

744

It seemed to me that the police report made me look like the negligent one. Why was the report filed on April 29 then altered on April 30th? I also had no idea who he had been with. I had only mentioned that I would assume it was one of his friends. I informed Harold of everything and he said he had to file another 51A because Evan had been in Dave's care when the incident occurred.

Exhibit Q: 51A April 30th, 2002
51A REPORT 4/30/2002 incident occurred on 4/17/02

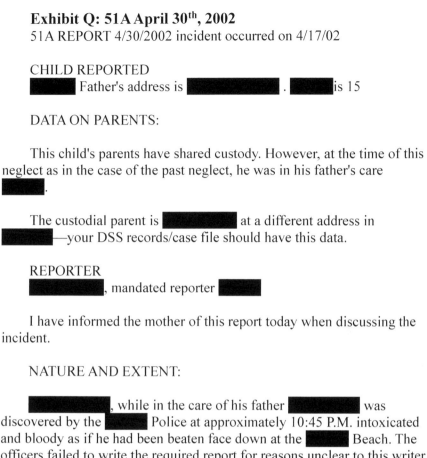

CHILD REPORTED
███████ Father's address is ████████████ . █████ is 15

DATA ON PARENTS:

This child's parents have shared custody. However, at the time of this neglect as in the case of the past neglect, he was in his father's care █████.

The custodial parent is ████████████ at a different address in ████████—your DSS records/case file should have this data.

REPORTER
████████████, mandated reporter ████████

I have informed the mother of this report today when discussing the incident.

NATURE AND EXTENT:

████████████, while in the care of his father ████████████ was discovered by the ████████ Police at approximately 10:45 P.M. intoxicated and bloody as if he had been beaten face down at the █████ Beach. The officers failed to write the required report for reasons unclear to this writer, the shift commander and his mother and the ████████████ Juvenile Court Probation Department. It would also appear that the report, when finally written, lacked certain data elements such as the apparent beating and other significant data as reported to me by the mother. At the time that he was taken to the ██████ Hospital he was discovered to have a BAC of .27%. He was in a ***blackout**** and unconscious. As a result of such a state of intoxication he has NO recall of the events leading up to that time nor much of what ensued after he was discovered.

AWARENESS OF INCIDENT:

I was informed several days after the incident. At that time it was the mother's plan to contact the ██████████ Juvenile Probation Department, which she did a few days ago. I felt that this 51A was appropriate and should be filed by me. This is the second time that Mr. ██████ has allowed his son to become intoxicated. In the previous 51A he had bought his son beer at a Crosby, Stills, Nash and Young concert in Boston—about a year or so ago.

ACTION:

The Probation Department has decided to again prosecute the alcoholic child as a delinquent—NOTE - AS A DELINQUENT, NOT AS A SUBSTANCE ABUSER/ALCOHOLIC - on Friday May 2, 2002. In a previous Court appearance when this substance abuser was mandated to the DYS facility in ██████ - he asked the judge to place him in a treatment facility and she responded with a sarcastic "Too late, take him away." As a result, he has only been afforded minimal treatment at the Gosnold facility for 10 days and then an outpatient program that was inappropriate for him but Court mandated - a Band-Aid at best.

OTHER INFORMATION:

To quote Shakespeare/Hamlet "there is something rotten in the State of Denmark." The juvenile Court system in ██████ is responsible for a poor and inept handling of this child for as long as he has been in their system. I am more worried about this child's future than I was my own children's recovery if we continue to allow this Court to make wrongful decisions concerning this child's safety, welfare and eventual recovery from his substance abuse pathology. They could have placed him into treatment on several occasions but did not for reasons that defy good logic and common sense. I am pleading with you to do whatever is necessary to insure that this child receive adequate, long-term treatment at a juvenile substance abuse treatment program such as the Gushing House in Dorchester, the Pegasus program in Haverhill and the Way Back in Attleboro. I am also sure that my last request on the 51A I filed before - that his visits with his father should only BE SUPERVISED VISITATION.

For whatever reason, DSS did not follow up on this last 51A. I can only speculate that they did not want to open the can of worms again after the last fiasco. After the last 51A determination, Dave had repeatedly stormed their office, threatened to sue them and have anyone involved fired. I can also imagine that Evan's age and the lack of backing from the court were a factor.

In the meantime, Dave wasted no time in bringing Evan to Mike, the counselor who I had only taken Evan to twice because of his affiliation with Dave. Even though Evan never had counseling with Mike again, Mike wrote a letter for Dave expressing Dave's concern over his son's alcohol abuse. Dave also wrote a letter to Harold, who had advocated so passionately for Evan, terminating Harold's services. Dave then coerced sixteen year old Evan into signing this letter.

EXHIBIT R: Evan Letter April 30, 2002

April 30th 2002

 & Associates

This letter is a follow up to my phone conversation with you last week. At that time I informed you that I no longer wish to be involved with you in counseling.

This shall serve as written notice that *I* no longer want you. ▮ & Associates or anyone affiliated with your office to be involved in counseling or any other capacity with me.

Sincerely,

Thankfully, this latest incident finally got Evan the rehabilitation that I had been fighting for. He was admitted to a program called the 'Road Back' in Attleboro for two months. Although Harold could no longer be actively involved in Evan's recovery, he did write letters to the program facilitators detailing what was going on with Evan and his concerns for him. He described Dave in an email to me as being "the biggest threat to Evan's sobriety."

Evan's counselor at the Road Back was a man barely in his twenties and Evan was only his second client. When I met with the young man he listened attentively to what I had to say and agreed with Harold and me regarding Evan's plight. That is, until he met with Dave.

I went to Attleboro every week to visit Evan but saw no improvement whatsoever. I was surprised to learn that Dave had also visited him and wondered what his angle was. Suddenly Evan was spewing his blame all over me. "Dad says it's your fault that I'm here. I don't need to be here. It's normal for kids my age to want to drink. I hate it and it's all your fault."

Evan came out of the Road Back program towards the end of summer vacation. Still mad at me, he decided to spend those few weeks with his father. I was at work when I got a call from the P.O. at Juvenile to tell me that Evan had tested positive for cocaine. Once again, he faced lock-up. This time he was sent to the Bxxxxx Detention facility until he could get accepted into another rehab center. Bxxxxx Detention was probably one of the best places that Evan had been to. It was no picnic, but the teenagers were treated with respect, something I certainly didn't see down at Juvenile Court.

Evan ended up spending over a month at Bxxxxx Detention. The feeling of walking in and seeing him escorted into the visitors' room with the other teens in orange jumpsuits was a reality slap in the face for me. Evan hadn't stolen cars or broken into houses, like many of his fellow 'inmates' - he had knocked his father's plants off the deck and violated his probation by not being able to abstain from drinking.

Evan was a conflicted teenager, not a criminal, yet he was confined like an animal. We were only allowed a minimal time for visiting, until a buzzer went off and then Evan was escorted back to his 'cell'. I'd look at him and the other young teens and wonder how different things might be for them if the facility focused not on their mistakes, but on discovering then encouraging their skills. If Evan could have just immersed himself in music and had been acknowledged for his abilities, it would have made a huge difference in how he dealt with his pain. I couldn't comprehend how Dave could use Evan's love for music against him.

Evan went from the detention center to Cushing House in Boston. It had the reputation of being one of the best juvenile rehabilitation programs available. I dropped Evan off with my prayers for his healing. He was not happy to be going to another rehab and demonstrated his anger with cold silence in the car.

I drove to Cushing House on Wednesdays for the parents support meetings, which Dave never attended. I liked what I heard. The stories were heartbreaking, but the program had its success stories. For the first time in a long time I had hope for Evan's recovery.

Evan was there less than two weeks when he called to tell me that he was being kicked out. He said he'd gotten into an argument with another resident and they'd exchanged racial epithets. The director had a zero-tolerance policy for the n-word. I was speechless. Evan had been showing some signs of genuine healing so I begged them to find another way to punish him. They would not relent. I reluctantly drove to Boston to bring my son home while silently praying that a seed had been planted during those two weeks.

At first it seemed as though my prayers had been answered. Evan was happy to be home and soon embroiled himself in his music. That is until Dave lured Evan back to his home by offering to let Evan have band practices in his finished basement.

One day, Evan asked to me go with him to his father's house to grab one of his amps that needed repair because it was too heavy for him to load into the car himself. I didn't want to go but Evan assured me that there was no chance of Dave, or anyone else, being home.

As I entered my old home, feelings and memories flooded my soul. Dave hadn't changed much in terms of the décor but the house felt very different; almost eerie. I checked over my shoulder several times as I followed Evan down the basement stairs to retrieve his amp. He showed me how Dave had set up a single bed behind the stairwell with a sheet hanging in front of it "for privacy" for when Evan stayed there. I glanced into the two bedrooms off the living area and noticed how they were full of Dave's many TV's and computers. I wondered how hard it would have been to clear them out so that Evan could have his own room. It sickened me to think of him sleeping behind the stairs. Evan was ecstatic, however, about his reunification with his father and was full of hope for better times.

The good always seemed to be followed by the bad as far as Evan and his father were concerned. One night, after Dave got mad at Evan for something, he dumped all Evan's music equipment outside in the rain. I remember Dave calling Evan to inform him of what he'd done and Evan frantically calling his friend and band member, Tim, to help him rescue his equipment.

"Please Tim, come over right away. All my equipment is in the rain," he'd pleaded, on the verge of tears. "We need your van to load it up and bring it to my mom's house. Hurry! Please!"

Tim came right over. The boys retrieved the wet equipment from Dave's yard and unloaded it into a small room in my home. Although it was hardly ideal, I let the boys hold practices in there. We had to shut all the windows in the summertime to stop the neighbor from calling the police because of the noise and, although we'd be roasting in the heat, it was good to see Evan enjoying his music.

Evan soon forgave his father for putting his music equipment out in the rain. By the fall of 2002, he was quickly falling back into his old habits. He spent more and more time with his father until I barely saw him at all. The few times that I did see him he was verbally abusive to me. His rage seemed to come out of him like a bodily function, as if he couldn't help himself. Evan was approaching adulthood and going to his father's house meant that he could drink and smoke.

I occasionally updated Harold and he and I both agreed that Evan still harbored hopes of getting something emotionally from Dave. I also believe that Evan felt he had to remove himself from me in order to stop hurting me. I could see it in his eyes. By the time he was 18 I rarely saw him. I wondered that if something were to happen to him, would anyone even tell me about it? On the few occasions that I did see him he had a look in his eyes that warned if he spent too much time around me, or if we tried to discuss anything, that he'd resort to the verbal abuse again.

Throughout all of this chaos with Evan, I still was trying to get full custody of Amy. Things were not good for her either.

Chapter 14

ATTEMPTS TO GET FULL CUSTODY OF AMY

I wished I could have cloned myself because I was torn in so many directions. It was clear that I was losing my youngest daughter. I couldn't even talk to her when she was staying at Dave's but during the short time that she was with me, he became more and more relentless about taking her to places on my time. I knew I didn't have to send her but he would get Amy so enthused on the phone call that if I tried to discourage her she would become hysterical. If she didn't do what he wanted, Dave would punish her or make her feel guilty. Her hysteria would also concern me and I worried that the stronger the stand I took, the harder he would be on her. I recalled many times when Evan would hysterically call me from his visitation with his father and ask me if he could come home. If I told him I'd come to get him, Dave would tell me, "I'm warning you D, if you try to take him home I will punish him severely."

If Amy had a rare day off from school and I tried to make plans with her, Dave would call and have something bigger and better for her to do. It usually involved Elizabeth and my baby grandson. Dave knew that Amy poured all her emotions into her nephew. He became her world and her escape from the madness. If Dave asked Amy to help Elizabeth with the baby and I dared object it only reinforced everything that Amy was being trained to believe about me.

Amy also loved her cheerleading. She was so good at it and we spent a lot of time at practices and cheerleading meets. She had a particular cheer that she and her friends had put together. After she showed it to me I was so impressed that I praised her with abandon. However, after she left for Dave's, I found a letter that had fallen on the floor. She'd written to Marla's daughter telling her how I'd criticized her demonstration as being 'unprofessional'. I was heartbroken to see that she felt she had to lie about me to stay in good graces with Dave and Marla.

I still spoke to Harold, Evan's former counselor, who repeatedly told me that as long as Dave had unsupervised access to our children nothing would improve. I had no reason to believe anything would change with this court but I had to keep trying. Amy was not in a healthy place and I knew that Dave would do anything to keep control over her.

One night, at around 9 pm, I called Amy at Dave's house. Amy answered and said she was home alone because her father had gone to a party. She didn't know what time he was coming back. I hated her being alone on that dark dead end street but I also knew she wouldn't come to my house. I asked her to at least call me when Dave got home. I called back hourly to check on her knowing that I couldn't sleep until I knew there was an adult with her. She was annoyed but promised to call me when he arrived.

Amy finally called me around midnight to say that her father had come home with rental movies for them to watch. She then started to giggle. I asked her why she was giggling. She replied "Dad is tickling me. I've got to go." Then she hung up.

I felt like I had been punched in the stomach as I flashed back over ten years to the memory of Dave straddling Elizabeth as he tickled her. Nausea flashed through my body. There was nothing I could do and no one who would help me. Feeling totally impotent I collapsed on the floor and sobbed myself to sleep.

I started the next day with a strong conviction to find an attorney who could help me get custody of Amy, no matter what it cost me. I had already spent so much on attorneys with nothing to show for it. The woman who had covered for my original attorney in the custody hearing had sent me a bill for $800 for her time in court with me. I'd already given my original attorney a retainer and didn't understand why I should have to pay her instead of him paying her. He explained that he'd already used up my retainer but if I called her office and explained my confusion he felt certain she would work something out with me. She refused and even though I sent her what I could, she still sent me the next bill with compounded interest. At this rate I'd never get the bill paid. I called again and the office manager said that the lawyer was unwilling to alter the billing. I wrote a letter stating I'd report her to the Bar and never received another bill.

Thanks to Independence House, I was able to get in touch with Wendy Murphy, a highly respected lawyer who did a lot of advocacy for women like me. She couldn't take my case but said she knew of a lawyer from outside of Boston named Beth Quack who was an expert in domestic abuse and custody issues. I called Beth's office, found out her fee and quickly made an appointment with her.

My first impression of her was that she was another arrogant attorney who spent most of my consultation talking about herself and her successes. Beth looked over the documentation in my case and felt we had 'real solid evidence' to win Amy back. That was all I needed to hear. She saw that in the year and a half of DSS involvement that Dave did nothing that was required of him. I, however, had I'd jumped through hoops. Even though I had already been going to Al-Anon and Independence House before DSS involvement, they required me to go to even more meetings several times a week. In all my years of Al-Anon, I'm the only person I know of who had to get signatures to prove that I was there. Although it was humiliating, I would have done anything that was asked of me to have Amy home and safe.

I was out straight between the four nights a week Al-Anon meetings, individual and group counseling twice a week at Independence House, trying to work and parent my at-risk-child, spend what little quality time I could with Amy and maintain all the other duties of single parenthood.

Dave, on the other hand, continued to do nothing. He also had assignments from DSS, one of them being to attend classes for abusers. He not only had refused to go, but he wouldn't talk to the DSS workers nor let them in his home.

Beth was sure this would carry immense weight in our request for Amy. She studied all the therapists' letters I'd received over the years which supported my sanity and my efforts to try to protect my children. They also outlined Dave as a classic abuser.

EXHIBIT S: Letters of Support 1999 - 2002
L█████ H████ P█████████ (1999)

L██████ H. P█████████ LMHC, LMFT

P.O. Box ████████ MA ████

May 1999

To Whom It May Concern:

I have known ██████████ for 5½ years. She started out as a group member in a men's + women's psychotherapy group and has been a member of an ongoing spiritual group before she moved to Western Mass; since she returned

████ has grown tremendously since I've known her. She is a deeply spiritual person and is always working hard at being the best that she can be. She is totally committed to her children and is extremely loving, understanding and emotionally available. She has weekly shared in the group I facilitate, her fears and concerns about her children's relationship with their father and his girlfriend. Despite often being seen as the "disgruntled ex-wife" she with the support + encouragement of the group, has been an outspoken advocate for her son, who has had many problems over the past few years.

████ is honest; has great integrity; She does not overreact nor does she exaggerate the truth. She is doing what I would hope any mother would do, and that base-line, is protecting her children from an extremely emotionally damaging situation.

I will willingly speak personally to anyone on her behalf. I urge you to listen very carefully to what she is saying and to think first + foremost of the emotional well-being of these children.

Sincerely,

**Counseling Services
& Associates
Main Street Unit 4
, Massachusetts**

c/o

Phone ( )

October 13, 2000 To Whom It May Concern:
We have seen ███████(age 14) in counseling on
a weekly basis since 6/99 and ███████ (age 12)
since 8/99 on the same schedule.

As of 10/7/2000, both children made good
progress in counseling and needed and wished to
continue with their present counselors. Their
mother supports this as the primary custodial
parent. Their father was invited to continue in
counseling, but did not. His criticism of myself
and both counselors ███████ ███████ and ███████
███████████ fits the pattern. This same pattern was
evident when the family lived in western
Massachusetts and sought help there. Mr. ███████ was
critical of the counselor there and wanted the
counselor removed. Mrs. ███████ can add to this.

Both children have been torn between their
parents because of this situation. Mrs. ███████ has
worked with us and supported our work with the
children. Mr. ███████ has attempted to undermine
and/or cut off any contact the children have with
their counselors as he did in the past. You will
see an example of that in his letters and faxes to
this office. On the other hand, you will see by the
mother's letter what counseling has meant to
███████, ███████ and for herself. The attorneys have
this correspondence.

167

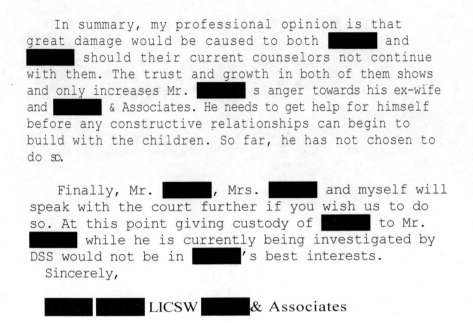

In summary, my professional opinion is that great damage would be caused to both ███ and ███ should their current counselors not continue with them. The trust and growth in both of them shows and only increases Mr. ███ s anger towards his ex-wife and ███ & Associates. He needs to get help for himself before any constructive relationships can begin to build with the children. So far, he has not chosen to do so.

Finally, Mr. ███, Mrs. ███ and myself will speak with the court further if you wish us to do so. At this point giving custody of ███ to Mr. ███ while he is currently being investigated by DSS would not be in ███'s best interests.
Sincerely,

███████ LICSW ███ & Associates

Independence House (March 22, 2001)

Independence House, Inc.

█████

█████ Massachusetts

█████

Tel. █████████

Fax: █████████

24-HOUR HOTLINE

1 800 439-6507

March 22, 2001

To Whom This May Concern,

    I am writing this letter in regards to Ms █████
█████ █████ has been a client of Independence House,
Inc. since May of 1999. I have had the pleasure of seeing
█████ for individual counseling since December of 2000
on a weekly basis. Prior to December, she was seen by
another staff member for individual counseling dating back
to May of 1999. █████ has had perfect attendance and has
always been punctual. She works very hard to advocate for
her children, and always has their best interest in mind. Ms.
█████ has done a great job of overcoming the abuse she
suffered in her marriage.
    At this time I regret that I will be leaving the agency,
but will see that █████ is matched with another counselor.
If you have any questions feel free to contact the agency at
the above number.

Sincerely,

█████████████

█████████████
Domestic Violence Counselor

169

She also read a letter from my counselor, D.K. stating that I displayed no signs of mental illness:

D.K. Letter, 2002

& Associates

Counseling, Program Development and Management

P. O. Box▮▮▮▮▮

▮▮▮▮▮, Massachusetts ▮▮▮

Phone ▮▮▮▮▮   Fax ▮▮▮▮▮

May 30, 2002

Re: ▮▮▮▮▮

To Whom It May Concern:

I have been doing supportive therapy with ▮▮▮▮▮ for three quarters of a year to help her sort out issues and challenges arising from the adversarial joint custody situation she finds herself in with her ex-husband.

In the time that I have known her, ▮▮▮▮▮ has shown herself to be a reliable, forthright, well spoken, and truthful person. She is fully competent and displays absolutely no mental problems or deficiencies of any kind.

In my estimation she is an excellent parent, showing compassion and caring for both of her minor children above and beyond that expected of any normal parent.

I will gladly furnish any additional information in this regard, if necessary.

Sincerely,

▮▮▮▮▮, MSW, LICSW

Beth went through Evan's files and noted the alcohol connection to his father. I did my part by collecting all my e-mails and copied everything for her. I did everything I could to make her job easier. I even had Lundy Bancroft, author of several books on abuse and controlling partners, ready to act on my behalf as my expert witness.

Mr. Bancroft was working with me and other women on what became the "Battered Mother's Testimony Project"; an intensive two-year statewide study of Probate Courts in Massachusetts that was sponsored by the women at Wellesley University. I had become involved with the project after seeing a notice posted at Independence House looking for women who'd had bad experiences in Probate Court. I briefly told them my story over the phone and was asked if I could travel out to Western Mass. to do an in-depth interview. Many stories like mine were pouring in to the Project about the Probate Courts across the state and Wellesley University decided to probe more deeply into them.

My interview lasted a few hours. I had to provide names, dates and documentation. After going to several meetings, I was asked to be one of five testifiers in a Human Rights Tribunal, scheduled on Mother's Day, 2002, at the State House in Boston. Wellesley created a ten-minute tape of the testimonies where we spoke before domestic abuse professionals and politicians. Mr. Bancroft was well aware of my case and wanted to help me in any way that he could. I was hopeful when he offered to be an Expert Witness.

Beth had felt certain of winning the case, although she cautioned that we were going up against a judge who had a reputation of not being fair or sensitive to the needs of children. She moved very slowly and I felt as though Amy was caught in a tidal wave that was pulling her out to sea. I didn't have time to sit on the shore and just watch. Beth did not respond well to my sense of urgency but she did secure us a date in May to go before Judge Terrible in Oceanside County Probate Court with our petition to regain full custody of Amy.

Despite our hopes of success, the judge was rude and abusive when he read over our petition for custody of Amy. He asked why we were "suddenly" coming in to change the orders. Beth explained that in the GAL Report Alicia had recommended that the custody arrangement stay the same while we were involved with DSS. Even though the head of the children's counseling agency had implored them not to, DSS had dropped the case. Beth was asking for a quick trial date.

Judge Terrible became very angry and yelled that in his courtroom things didn't work that way; that he had a full roster and we would have to wait for several months. I knew how hypocritical that statement was after hearing about fathers who'd had trial days set for them in as little as two weeks.

The judge gave us a date in July. Lundy Bancroft couldn't make the July date. Beth and I both felt that he was crucial to the case so we asked for a later date. The next trial date we could get wasn't until October. Over the last year and a half I hadn't spent one weekend with Amy. I prayed for the day that I wouldn't have to see her shuffled between homes like a piece of property.

October 14th couldn't come quickly enough.

Chapter 15

HOPE

After two years of preparing, and paying Beth $3,000 for her services, the trial date finally arrived. Beth continually reaffirmed what a strong case we had but always added that given the judge's tendencies it may not be enough to win. She repeatedly said we would immediately appeal the ruling, if need be, and that she had enormous confidence in an appeal. She felt that if we went before a different judge her appeal skills would be successful.

Our trial was scheduled for 9 am. Everything was in place. Lundy Bancroft had traveled from Western Mass. and was ready to give his expert testimony. DSS representatives were also ready to testify. Nadine, from the Domestic Violence Unit of the Oceanside Police Station, was there to support me and there was even a reporter from the local newspaper ready to cover the story.

Elizabeth stood beside Dave. I wondered why Amy's court appointed lawyer, who had previously said that she couldn't talk to me or Dave about the case because she was Amy's lawyer, now sat in court next to Dave. I asked Beth to make an issue of this but she waved me off.

Judge Terrible had a full courtroom by the time our case was called. The lawyers went up to his bench and Judge Terrible loudly proclaimed, "I do not understand why you have to have a trial. Amy has made her choice to continue with shared custody."

I overheard my lawyer say that there were "mitigating circumstances" and that we did indeed have to go to trial. The judge was clearly irritated and bellowed, "If you insist on going through with this then you will have to wait for this courtroom to clear out first!"

By the time the courtroom cleared out it was 3 pm. Every one there to testify on my behalf had expected a morning trial and Mr. Bancroft had to leave after waiting for several hours. DSS couldn't stay either. There was only time for one witness to be heard.

The lawyers put Alicia Pustule on the stand. Dave's lawyer was the first to question her and asked Alicia if she knew why Elizabeth's father Ron and I had broken up, decades earlier. Alicia said she understood that it was because I fought with him constantly.

The truth was that Elizabeth's father and I were only together for a very short time when Elizabeth was a baby and we rarely fought. The few times he had visited Elizabeth I'd been friendly and even invited him in for dinner for the sake of our daughter. I'd always felt that as hard as things had been for me, he was the one on the losing end because he'd missed out on the experience of raising our beautiful Elizabeth. In addition to this lawyer's bias, I was even more concerned about why this brief relationship from twenty-five years ago was even being brought up in court.

Beth cross-examined Alicia and many things started to come out. My lawyer brought up things that Alicia had been made aware of, like the time that Dave had encouraged Amy to belly dance in a local coffee house that also served alcohol. Alicia replied that she "didn't recall" this. Beth also asked Alicia if she was aware that Dave had taken a naked video of Amy. Again, she replied, "I don't recall."

With every question Beth spun at her Alicia could only repeat her mantra of "I don't recall."

Judge Terrible had squirmed on the bench as he shifted positions and tapped his pencil. The back of Dave's neck turned blood red and his angry vein in his forehead had started to bulge. A friend of mine in the courtroom said she was certain that he was going to either explode or implode with rage. I could feel his anger pulsating from his body. Judge Terrible had heard enough and quickly called for a recess. It would have been evident to anyone in the courtroom, had there been anyone left, that the court had screwed up in a major way by placing custody of this child with Dave.

The trial was scheduled to continue on Nov. 14, 2002. I felt real hope and confidence in my lawyer and that, no matter how begrudgingly, the judge would have no choice but to place Amy back in my full custody.

Chapter 16

HOPE CRUSHED

I anxiously awaited the end of this trial as I imagined all the things Amy and I would be able to do together. I would tuck her in to bed at night, brush her hair and hold her close. I'd look forward to listening to her teenage chatter about her latest best friend or boy crush. According to Beth, the odds (and the facts) were in my favor in spite of the judge's obvious bias. However, she always reassured me that in the smallest of chances that we didn't succeed in this court room, she would rally in an appeal in Boston.

A few weeks before the trial resumed I felt a shift in Beth. Dave had sent me an e-mail saying that he would continue paying me child support if I agreed to continue with shared custody. This was laughable. Through all the years of court-ordered child support Dave had rarely paid and was thousands of dollars in arrears. I realized that he desperately did not want this trial to continue. After relaying the e-mail to me, Beth shocked me by asking me to consider Dave's offer. I shot back an email, "Are you kidding? How can you ask me that?" This didn't make any sense to me. Beth knew that there was no such thing as "shared custody" with Dave. In the past year and a half I'd had no leverage as a parent and was continually shut out by Dave. Beth knew this and had assured me that we would not enter any agreements with Dave because he didn't honor agreements. The goal all along was full legal and physical custody. She was suddenly acting and speaking differently but I couldn't put my finger on why.

Lundy Bancroft could not make the November 14th court date but DSS was there again. Elizabeth showed up with Dave and my cousin Gina, who had been subpoenaed by Dave's lawyer even though she had no relevance to the case. I felt a pit in my stomach when I turned a corner and saw Dave sitting on a bench outside the courtroom flanked by each of them.

I tried to shake off the pain I felt as I made my way through the doors of the courtroom to the people who would be there to support me.

I sat with my friend Mary, Paula and her teenage son who had come to support me. Beth let me know right away that it was standard protocol to try to negotiate an agreement before trial. I thought that had already been done and we would just pick up where we'd left off in October. Beth and I had already discussed a 'no negotiations' approach many times over the past two years. Dave did not uphold court orders so there was no point in trying to negotiate them. Beth said okay and walked away.

After waiting for close to an hour for Beth's return I got up to search for her. I peeked into Judge Hatcher's courtroom and saw her sitting with Dave's lawyer, Alicia Pustule and Amy's lawyer. I had thought I was supposed to be a part of these proceedings. I was tempted to interrupt but had a feeling that the court officer outside the door wouldn't allow that. Besides, at this point, I still felt, or hoped that Beth was there to help me.

Beth remained in the courtroom for what seemed to be another hour. The doors were shut and it was clear that this was a private meeting. When she finally came out she stunned me by asking me to agree to terms that had been set out by Dave's attorney. I was horrified when I read the terms. There was nothing in them that was favorable to me or to my children. I responded with an empathic "NO!!!" Beth asked me what I didn't agree to and I almost screamed, "All of it!" She looked disgusted as she went back into the courtroom, shutting the door behind her.

I went to sit on a bench to wait for Beth to reappear. Another half hour had passed before I went looking for her again. I found the courtroom was empty and the court officer told me that my lawyer was in Judge's Terrible's Chambers. I began to get that panicky feeling that I'd had during my divorce proceedings when I'd realized that I was done for. Beth Quack was my lawyer but I couldn't even keep track of where she was or what she was doing on my behalf.

Beth eventually emerged from the judge's chambers and walked over to me with determination written all over her face. She warned me that I could lose all contact with my children if I didn't sign the proposed custody agreement. It was her professional opinion that there was no way this court would allow me full custody. I felt sucker-punched and refused to agree to continue shared custody of Amy.

Returning to Judge Terrible's courtroom, I sat with my little support group. Nadine, from the DV unit of the police department, had shown up and sat quietly beside me. She would occasionally pat my hand or rub my back. She didn't seem to have words that could comfort me, but her support was felt deeply.

I was disoriented as Beth's words swam in my head, "The judge is not going to allow this trial to continue. You are going to lose all custody if you don't sign the agreement. There are no grounds for appeal. This is it. You will lose both your children." She had reversed everything she'd been telling me for the last two years. I just wanted to get out of there. I was once again dead in the water in this courtroom with no one to stand on my behalf. Beth tried to redeem herself by promising me the agreement would stipulate that the children would have to get counseling and that the court psychologist, Dr. K., would be in charge of recommending councilors and would make sure that the children attended all counseling sessions. Had I been in the right state of mind, I would have remembered that the court psychologist was the same man who'd put in writing a few years earlier that Dave and I could not successfully manage 'shared custody'.

Beth also said Dr. K. would provide the counselors with all the pertinent documentation, including the letter Lundy Bancroft had written. To my knowledge, Mr. Bancroft's expert testimony was never reviewed by the judge.

EXHIBIT T: Expert testimony regarding my case
Lundy Bancroft
Family Issues Specialist

P.O. Box xxxxx Northampton, MA 01061 xxxxx

December 5, 2001
Attorney ███████ Brockton MA 02301

Dear Attorney███,
The following is a report I am submitting in preparation for the expert testimony I intend to provide in the ███ matter. The report reviews my qualifications (my curriculum vitae is also attached), summarizes the testimony I expect to give and the basis for that testimony, lists my expected compensation, and lists other cases in which I have provided expert testimony.

QUALIFICATIONS

I am a domestic violence expert with fifteen years of experience in the field, specializing in men who batter and their children. I have worked with over 2000 batterers as a counselor and supervisor, and now serve as a Guardian ad Litem, Care and Protection Investigator, and expert witness in cases involving allegations of domestic violence or child abuse. My first book *The Batterer as Parent: Addressing the Impact of Domestic Violence on Family Dynamics* is forthcoming in March from Sage Publications, and my second book *Why Does He Do That? Inside the Minds of Angry and Controlling Men* is forthcoming in September from Penguin Putnam. I have been training judges, probation officers, and other court personnel for eight years, and have been a regular presenter for DSS, DTA, DOR, DPH, OCCS, the Attorney General's office, the state police, and local police departments. I have also consulted regularly to Massachusetts General Hospital on domestic violence perpetrators, My guide "Assessing Risk to Children from Unsupervised Visitation with flatterers" is distributed nationally by the National Council of Juvenile and Family Court Judges. My articles have also been published in the *New England Journal of Medicine, Journal of Contemporary Psychology*, and *Domestic Violence Report*, and I am co-author of two nationally-marketed curricula, one for working with batterers and one for teen dating violence education in schools.

I recently completed a six-month study for the Massachusetts Department of Public Health on addressing the effects on children of exposure to domestic violence. In addition, I periodically evaluate state-certified batterer programs for the Department of Public Health. My curriculum vitae is attached.

OPINIONS TO WHICH I EXPECT TO TESTIFY IN THE MATTER

1) That the profile, characteristics, and behavior patterns of male batterers have been well-established and are widely accepted and recognized by both mental health and legal professionals. That this established profile includes the following characteristics, among others: a repeating pattern of coercive and intimidating behaviors; volatility often accompanied by retaliatory behavior when a relationship ends; retaliatory behavior when the woman seeks assistance or makes other efforts to stop the abuse; using children as a weapon against the victim; chronic dishonesty; using custody and visitation litigation as a form of abuse; and other distinguishing attitudes and behaviors.

My description of the male batterer is drawn from my very extensive clinical experience, from my own published works, and from published works by Jeff Edleson, Edward Gondolf, David Sonkin, Peter Jaffe, Robert Geffner, Neil Jacobson, John Gottman, Donald Dutun, Michael Paymar, Ellen Pence, Richard Tolman, Jay Silverman, and others.

2)That it is very common for male batterers to create profound divisions with families, often including efforts to alienate one or more of the children from their mother or to turn siblings against each other. That a batterer who engages in such behaviors typically uses tactics such as conditioning the children to think badly of their mother, rewarding children for disrespectful or defiant behavior towards their mother, making false statements about one family member to another, and abusing or humiliating the mother in front of the children.

My description of these family dynamics is drawn from my experience as detailed above, and from published works by Peter Jaffe, Robert Geffner, David Hurley, Janet Johnston, Linda Campbell, Jacquelyn Campbell, Maria Roy, and others.

3) That there is a high overlap between battering behavior and violation of children's sexual boundaries, particularly towards girls. Further, that some useful indicators have been established of which batterers are most likely to engage in these types of boundary violations.

My description of this overlap is drawn from my experience as detailed above, and from published works by Gregory Paveza, David Finkelhor, Laura McCloskey, Judith Herman, Janet Johnston, Linda Campbell, Anna Salter, and others.

4) That exposure to domestic violence is often traumatizing to children. Further, that the necessary factors for children to heal well from such exposure are well-established. Finally, that extensive unsupervised contact with the battering parent can interfere with such a healing process, even in cases where the child states a desire for such contact.

My description of trauma and healing in children exposed to domestic violence is drawn from my own published works, and from published works by Peter Jaffe, Jeff Edleson, Einat Peled, Robbi Rossman, Honore Hughes, Mindy Rosenberg, Jill Davis, Betsy McAlister Groves, Sandra Graham-Bermann, and others.

5) That custody evaluators (such as Guardians ad Litem) nationwide often fail to be adequately trained in the profile, tactics, and parenting characteristics of male batterers, and often do not adequately consider the implications of these characteristics in shaping their recommendations regarding custody and visitation. That national standards for proper custody evaluation in the context of domestic violence allegations are in the process of being established, which gives further indication of the widely-recognized gaps that currently exist in this area.

My description of proper and improper custody and visitation evaluation in the context of domestic violence allegations is drawn from my own experience as detailed above, my published works, and from published works by Peter Jaffe, Robert Geffner, Massachusetts State Senator Cheryl Jacques, the National Council of Juvenile and Family Court Judges, Clare Dalton, and others.

COMPENSATION FOR THIS TESTIMONY (removed by author)

PREVIOUS APPEARANCES AS EXPERT WITNESS (removed by author)

Sincerely,

Lundy Bancroft (signature)

Lundy Bancroft
Family Issues Specialist

Feeling beaten up and defeated I signed the agreement which stated that we would alternate custody of not only Amy but also of Evan, who was never previously mentioned in any of our custody issues. Nadine broke her silence and looked in my eyes as she sadly told me "You didn't have a choice."

We stood before Judge Terrible with our new agreement in hand. As he scanned the agreement, he came to the part about the counseling. He smugly announced, "Dr. K will not be able to do that. He's being sent to Iraq." As there was no replacement for Dr. K this deleted the only small piece of comfort that I had in the whole ordeal.

I suspected that my lawyer had been massively pressured into getting me to sign the custody agreement. After I recuperated from this huge loss I asked Beth for my files. They contained a letter she'd received from Dave's attorney that was full of veiled threats regarding her bar status, referencing another case Beth was representing at the same time. The case was similar to mine and had brought her notoriety when it made front page and TV news. It was also under Judge Terrible's jurisdiction. I believe that Beth sacrificed me and my children to gain ground on this other case.

My hopes of getting custody of Amy came crashing down with a speed I couldn't have imagined. Not only had Beth betrayed me, but the vision of Elizabeth and my cousin Gina sitting on either side of Dave is burned into my memory. Most of all, I felt that I had betrayed myself and my children. I had nothing left. Everyone supporting me said I had no choice but to accept the situation.

The truth is, I wish I had stood up and screamed at the top of my lungs for justice. I wish to God that I had spoken my truth. I let them beat me down, but it taught me a huge lesson. Never again.

For the next six months Amy lived week-to-week between households. It was excruciating to see her pack her bags to go back and forth between three streets. This custody agreement was supposed to be 'better' by giving me a full week instead of three week days, but what didn't change was Dave's relentless manipulation to try to keep Amy with him whenever possible during my week. It didn't matter that it was against the court order. Dave didn't obey court orders and the court refused to enforce them. He always had a reason, usually related to Elizabeth and my grandsons, to come and get her. I knew it was only a matter of time before I lost her altogether.

Chapter 17

BROKEN HEART, BROKEN SOUL

I almost hit bottom, lost in the depths of depression that Dave was always accusing me of. It took me a few months to pull myself out of the pit of blackness, although I never fully recovered. I felt like a zombie at my Al-Anon meetings, clinging to any words that could ease my aching heart and soul.

Amy and I did have a chance to spend some quality time together at one of her cheerleading meets when we carpooled to Rhode Island with one of Amy's cheerleading friends and her mother. Amy was very excited, and I was thrilled to see her so excited about an event that included me.

We got up at 5 am in order to meet up at the designated area. We stopped for breakfast and had had a great time chatting in the car. I helped Amy with her hair and outfit before she went off to join her team. The other mother, Annie, was meeting up with her family so I found myself a seat high in the bleachers.

I noticed Dave stroll in and sit on a front bleacher not too far from me. Shortly after, Elizabeth and Carl joined him. They saw me and shot me a quick glance, but that was it. I sat through the whole competition alone without any further acknowledgment from my daughter or son-in-law.

Amy's team came in first place. I cheered and wanted to cry for joy. I ran down to congratulate her but Dave, Elizabeth and Carl got to her first. Amy glanced in my direction but then she ignored me. Dave, Elizabeth and Carl took pictures with Amy as I stood in the background, like a ghost. I felt invisible again. Amy only talked to me long enough to inform me that she was leaving with her father. I left with Annie and we travelled home with her daughter in an awkward silence.

We had entered the last custody agreement in November of 2002. In June of the following year, Elizabeth had sprained her ankle. She and Dave decided that Amy should live with her for the summer to help her out. No one asked me. Amy went straight from Dave's house to Elizabeth's. She called to tell me that she wouldn't be spending any time with me because her sister needed her.

Dave then made the unilateral decision that his child support was over, including the huge arrears I was owed, because Amy wasn't living with me for the summer. I took him to court in June, 2003 on contempt for failing to pay. We met with one of the officers of the court and he asked Dave why he wasn't paying child support. Dave explained that both children were living with him. Evan had been with him for a couple of months but had not moved out of my home. Amy had only been staying at Elizabeth's to help her out. The officer said that until Dave filed a Motion for Modification for change of custody he still had to obey the current order. Dave handed me a hundred dollars to appease the court officer and then left. The officer assured me that Dave had an obligation for weekly child support until he filed for modification and went before a judge. Part of me was relieved, but part of me knew that Dave wasn't going to do anything he didn't want to do.

I went back to court in August. Dave had still not paid anything since June. The court waited for Dave to show up but he was nowhere to be found. Coincidently, Judge Terrible wasn't on the bench that day. I had taken the day off from work and asked the sitting judge what my options were. He said I could take out a capias (warrant), which I did. Even though Dave lived and owned a business in town no one ever served him or brought him in on contempt.

The following day I was at work when I got a phone call from the court asking me to come in because Dave was there. The court officer told me that Dave had got his dates mixed up. Judge Terrible was back on the bench. I could not leave work so another date was made for the following week.

We appeared before Judge Terrible at the end of August. He asked Dave why he wasn't paying child support and Dave claimed that both the kids were only living with him. I told the Judge that I was maintaining a three bedroom home for the children and that their things were still all at my house. I also explained that Amy was spending the summer helping her sister recover from an injury. I reminded him that we still had joint custody and that Dave had been in arrears long before these recent agreements. I also added that no one had informed me that the children were planning to leave my home.

Dave announced to the judge, "The children don't want to be with their mother anymore and want little to do with her."

Judge Terrible seemed happy to take Dave's word and my Contempt hearing became Dave's Complaint for Modification for Custody, even though he hadn't even filed for it. Dave looked at the judge and with his sincerest and kindest voice said, "Your honor, I would be willing to give her $600 of what I owe her today." Dave owed me thousands at that point so $600 was a drop in the bucket. I also could not keep losing work to come into court once a month to beg for what was owed to me.

Although Dave claimed that he was willing to give me the money, he said he didn't have any cash and would have to write a check. I told the judge I would not accept a check because they always bounced. Judge Terrible barked at me, "Guess you will have to wait here until he goes to the bank then!"

Once we were outside the courtroom Dave pulled a wad of cash out of his pocket and peeled off $600 in cash right in front of the court officer. He handed it to me without saying a word but he glared at me with his 'cat who ate the mouse' grin. The court officer witnessed the whole thing but didn't bat an eye. It was clear to me that Dave's refusal to pay child support and carry insurance for his children was a non-issue to this court. Once again, Judge Terrible had taken Dave's word for gospel and ignored anything I had to say. Once again, Dave wasn't scolded for wasting the court's time or for not showing up when he was supposed to. However, above all that was Dave's words ringing in my head "The children don't want to be with their mother anymore."

I couldn't believe that Amy wasn't coming home. I cried all the way home then called her to ask if it was true. "I'm tired of going back and forth," she replied. I reminded her that I had fought against that arrangement because I'd known it was going to be so hard on her. She had nothing else to say.

It seemed that with every month, every year, I was losing ground. I was always losing something or someone. My pain was so deep that I felt it in my very bones. Every day I came home to the stillness and emptiness of my children's absence. I would often go into their rooms and smell their blankets or the clothes they'd left behind. I could hear their laughter and their squabbles as I stared at Evan's Jimmy Hendrix or Amy's Green Day posters. I ached for the intimacy I shared with Elizabeth and craved to hold my new grandson.

I had lost all three of my children and could only sit on the edges of their beds and wonder why. In my grief, I composed a poem entitled The Live Ghost. That's how I felt. I was alive but flitted around like a specter in my children's lives. I wasn't acknowledged as their mother and had to pinch myself to be sure that I still existed.

THE LIVE GHOST

I think I died and no one told me.
I'm in my home with no children. I see their rooms.
I see their clothes and music and beds, but I don't see them.
I go to every event important to my children like school open houses, recitals, gym meets, just as I always have. Only now I float around on the periphery and they don't seem to see me.
I'm trying to get noticed but can't.
It's like being in a nightmare where you are screaming but no one hears you.
Christmas and Thanksgiving I walk the beach and I remember happy holidays; asking Elizabeth what pies to bring, getting gifts ready and savoring Christmas morning.
There is celebrating going on in my former marital home, with my former husband, my former in-laws and my children, but I am no longer part of it.

Not there, not anywhere.
I am trying to stay alive and fighting to change that.
No one hears my voice. I am trying to be heard.
I'm trying to say I need to protect, nurture and be part of my
children's lives.
What little I am able to get out falls on deaf ears. Mostly, I am
silenced.
No one seems to see me or hear me.
I realize that I did die. As a parent, I was murdered.
As a mother, I'm left with only memories.

In the fall, Amy had an open house at the high school. I went, not because I was informed, but because I already knew about it. Dave had instructed the high school to send all correspondence to him. I'd asked the school to send me copies too. They said I'd have to get a court order because I wasn't the custodial parent. Dave had misinformed the administration that he was now the only custodial parent. He even had the audacity to call me and ask me what childhood diseases Amy had had and for her immunization records.

I arrived at the open house with a heavy heart. As I approached Amy's first class Dave and Elizabeth walked in before me. They introduced themselves to the teacher and presented like they were father and mother, instead of father and sister. I came in behind them and sat on the sidelines. When I finally talked to the teacher I realized that I knew next to nothing of what was going on in my child's life. I wanted to be there. I needed to be there. But I felt like an intruder; an outsider who was floating over the crowd while Dave and Elizabeth were informed and deferred to.

It was so painful that at one point I passed Elizabeth in the hallway and grabbed her by the elbow. "Elizabeth, what are you doing? I'm Amy's Mom!!!" Dave had rushed over and yanked her away from me bellowing, "Don't talk to her!"

By November, I still had very little contact with Amy and I was getting desperate. I talked to another mom going through a similar nightmare and she suggested that I petition the court for Reintegration Therapy with my children. I took her advice and the petition was scheduled the day of my monthly Contempt Review. Dave was still not making child support payments despite the court's order.

EXHIBIT U: Motion for reintegration therapy with my children

Commonwealth of Massachusetts
The Trial Court
Probate and Family Court Department

Division _____   Docket No. _____

_____
Plaintiff/Petitioner

v.

_____
Defendant/Respondent

MOTION FOR

indeependent clinician to work with mother-child Relationship with the goal of Re-unification.

Now comes _____, the plaintiff/defendant/petitioner/respondent,
(name of moving party)

in this action who moves this Honorable Court as follows: _to obtain an independent clinician to aid in Reintegration with myself and my children due to parental alienation. I would ask the court to assist me in healing the mother-child Relationship which is so crucial for mental health. I would also ask the court to demand no interference from father and in fact Require his assistance in getting the children to therapy._

NOTICE OF HEARING

This Motion will be heard at the Probate & Family

Court in _____
(city)

on _November 6, 2003_
(month/day/year)

at _9:00 AM_
(time of hearing)

_____ (signature)

_____ (PRINT name)

_____ (street address)

_____ (city or town) _M.A._ (state) _____ (zip code)

Date: _____   Tel. No. ( )_____

The within motion is hereby **ALLOWED** – **DENIED.**

_____
Date

_____
Justice of the Probate and Family Court

INSTRUCTIONS

1. Generally, refer to Mass.R.Civ.P./Mass.R.Dom.Rel.P. 5, 6 and 7; Probate Court Rules 6, 29, and 29B.
2. If the opposing party is represented by an attorney who has filed an appearance, service of this motion MUST be made on the attorney.
3. Certificate of Service on Reverse side must be completed.
4. All motions shall be accompanied by a proposed order which shall be served with the motion.

CJ-D 400 (6/00)

I went before Judge Terrible with my Motion for Counseling. He appeared irritated with me and quickly denied the motion without even giving me a chance to speak. He added that he was also canceling the Contempt Review hearing on that day and all future hearings on the matter. I walked out of court having been denied counseling with my children and not being able to try to claim all the money owed to me. I later learned that Dave had filed a new Complaint for Modification requesting full custody of Amy. If I barely saw her with our Joint Custody arrangement, the thought of his being awarded full custody was like a bullet to my head.

We had a date set for February 2004 for Dave's Modification request for full custody. I refused to agree to give up Amy which meant it would have to go to trial. In the meantime I talked to a lawyer and was told that because child support was involved I was entitled to a Discovery in which Dave would have to disclose all his income and assets. Previous attempts to get a Discovery from Dave had failed. No lawyer was willing to spend the time to pursue it because of my limited funds. I knew in my heart that no one would represent me with the passion that I would have in representing myself. Besides, I had nothing left to lose.

I wrote up a proposal to Dave and his lawyer advising them that I would give up the thousands of dollars in back child support owed to me in exchange for continued shared custody of Amy and Evan. As bad as shared custody was, it was the last thread I had to hang on to my children.

After a few months, when I did not receive the Discovery I needed in order to proceed with the trial, I filed a motion with the court asking for more time until I received it. At the hearing Dave's lawyer told the judge that a Discovery wasn't needed.

Judge Terrible considered me with his usual disdain and annoyance. "Why do you think you should get a Discovery?" he snarled.

I was done with unscrupulous lawyers. I was done with being pushed around. I looked the judge square in the eyes and summoned my strength and confidence. Without ever taking my eyes off him I declared, "I want a Discovery because I know it's my legal right to have one." It felt like the equivalent of a show down. I could see the judge realized that he'd pushed me too far. I was ready to die for my cause.

Judge Terrible told Dave to have a Discovery ready for me by the end of the week. Dave and his lawyer looked shell shocked. They gathered up their briefcases and slunk out of the courtroom. With every step I took behind them I felt the power of my conviction, no longer afraid to speak up.

Dave did not provide the Discovery so I e-mailed him and told him that I was prepared to go back into court to get it. Suddenly he wanted to negotiate the deal I'd offered him a few months before he'd first approached the court with full custody. I had agreed to never pursue past due child support again if he dropped his motion. At the time he'd just laughed. This time he said he would have his lawyer "draw something up."

I replied, "No, *I* will draw something up."

Dave and his lawyer went back and forth with me trying to keep Dave in control but I would not back down. I wrote up the stipulation exactly as I wanted it and would settle for nothing less. As much as they tried to slick up the wording I would not let them. I felt strong and had nothing left to lose. They knew that I was at the point of no return.

EXHIBIT V: Stipulation of Agreement
COMMONWEALTH OF
MASSACHUSETTS

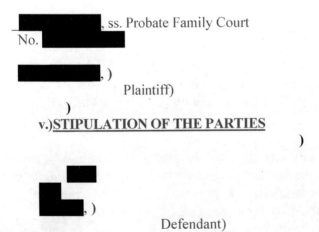

, ss. Probate Family Court

No.

,)

Plaintiff)

)

v.)<u>STIPULATION OF THE PARTIES</u>

)

,)

Defendant)

NOW COME the parties, ██████████ **and** ██████
██████, in the above entitled matter and hereby stipulate as
follows:

1.   The parties agree to continue shared physical
and legal custody of their daughter, ████████████.

2.   The parties agree that ████████ is to spend time
living with both parents during the course of each month.
Because they live within close proximity of one other,
transportation between houses is not an issue. The amount of
time spent at each residence shall be at the discretion of
████████. Neither party shall disparage the other and shall
encourage the sharing of visitation and overnights at
both houses.

3.   The parties agree to waive any past or future
claims for payment of alimony and child support between one
another. This includes the forgiveness of any arrearages for
either child support or alimony ████████████ is waving
her claims in order to continue with shared physical custody.

4.   In the event that either ████████ or ████████ need
a ride someplace, ████████████, as their mother, shall be
contacted by ████████ and given first option to transport
them. In the event that they are with ████████ and need a ride,
████████ will be the first person called by ████████.

5.   Should either party wish to take one or both
of the children out of the
Commonwealth of Massachusetts for a vacation, the other party
shall be notified
so as to have knowledge of where the children are and how they
can be reached
by telephone.

6.   Should either child have a medical emergency while
in the physical custody of
one of the parties, he or she shall forthwith notify the other party
concerning the
child's medical status, treatment and location.

7.   The parents of the children agree to encourage both
████████████ and ████████ to call and/or visit their grandparents, on
both sides of the family, especially on
holidays and birthdays.

8.   The parties agree to inform and consult with one
another on all major events in
the lives of their children.

In all other respects, all past orders of the court remain in full force and effect.

, Pro Se

Dated:

, Esq.

Attorney for

Dated:

I was aware that this new stipulation wasn't worth the paper it was written on but I wanted it in writing anyway. It was my legacy of what I had to go through to try to keep a connection with my children. I insisted that it say that in return for my giving up all the money I was owed that we would continue with shared custody, be informed of the children's whereabouts, and that the children be allowed to be reached by phone. I also made sure that it said that both parties be informed about medical issues and treatments. I wrote that the other parent be given first option if one of the children needed a car ride somewhere. I tried to include everything that Dave hadn't been doing.

Although he signed it, Dave never honored anything in the agreement. I never expected him to. There was no trial, and even if there were, and even if I'd had a great lawyer I know that it wouldn't have mattered. Facts didn't matter in this court. The mother-child bond didn't matter in this court. All that mattered was money, power, and influence, no matter the cost to the children or the other parent.

I felt bloody and beaten, but at the same time I felt like a Phoenix Rising. This pain would either kill me or motivate me to try to make changes in the system that had allowed me to lose my children. I was not the same person as when this nightmare started. As long as I fought for my children I had felt like I was treading on egg shells, afraid to anger Dave and the judges. That was over. My children were gone. I had to find a way to go on.

Janis Joplin's words rang in my head, "Freedom's just another word for nothing left to lose."

No more walking on egg shells.

I immediately filed a complaint against the Oceanside Probate Court with the Massachusetts Judicial Committee in Boston. They actually investigated my complaint instead of dismissing it, as they did with most of the people I knew who had filed similar complaints. However, the committee decided that there was no wrong conduct even though I had provided extensive documentation. The committee claimed that after "talking to witnesses" (court personnel) and reviewing the files there was no basis for the complaint. I later found that very few complaints are looked into and even fewer are upheld. It was "the fox guarding the hen house" scenario. There was no way for me to appeal this finding in Massachusetts because the Judicial Committee is the highest authority and probate courts are only regulated within their own state.

My disappointment turned to anger which I then used as fuel. I wrote a letter to The League of Women Voters about mothers losing custody in court and nobody caring. I also wrote to the local newspaper but the editor refused to publish it. I then wrote to the ACLU and the Whitehouse but was told there was nothing they could do.

The newspaper did publish coverage of a gala event that honored eight probation officers from probate courts across the state. One of them was Alicia Pustule. She was described as an 'unsung hero'.

Chapter 18

AFTERMATH

May 2004

I missed seeing Evan all dressed up for his prom. My heart melted when, months later, someone showed me his prom picture. It pierced my heart to not have been included in that milestone. I did attend his high school graduation and I cried with love and pride. Evan had had such a struggle in school but he'd made it.

After graduation, I didn't hear from Evan for months. He finally did contact me when he became addicted to drugs. He told me that he was in a very bad way and that he'd told his sisters. They had encouraged him to go to their father for help but Evan said his father's first reaction was to tell him to "suck it up." Elizabeth intervened and managed to get Dave to agree to pay for 8 days of detox on the condition that Evan pay him back. The detox only served to detox Evan physically and it was only a matter of weeks before he was back in the hell hole of addiction.

Evan told me that he believed he could only beat his addiction with methadone treatments. I came up with the $500 down payment for the methadone clinic and paid the program cost of $130 a week. I also shared my car with him so that he could make his daily trip to the clinic. I'd been saving for another car and decided to buy one prematurely so that Evan could have my old car.

Dave kept track of every penny he spent on Evan. At 19, Evan owed his father $6,000 for the initial detox program, community college fees and car repair costs following an accident. Dave expected Evan to pay his debt immediately; not once Evan got back on his feet which he was desperately trying to do. Evan went to the methadone clinic daily, he attended four classes in school and he worked hard. Instead of encouraging his son during this recovery period, Dave tried to sabotage him at every turn.

Evan could never do anything right in Dave's eyes. When Evan got mad at his father he told me things that made my blood run cold. He confirmed that all my worst nightmares and suspicions over the last few years had been true. Evan admitted to me that he had done drugs with his father's current girlfriend who, according to Evan, was horribly abusive to Amy. He also told me that Dave was always kicking him out of the house but Evan was never sure if Dave really meant it or if he was so drunk that he didn't realize what he was saying. Evan recounted nights when he'd come home to find Dave passed out drunk on the other side of the locked door. No amount of banging on the door, calling his father on the phone or yelling could wake him up so Evan would have to sleep in his car.

I learned from Evan that Dave was never home; especially on the weekends. "Dad's been leaving Amy alone since she was twelve." I asked Evan what the appeal was of living in a house with such trauma and chaos. He replied that it was because drama only happened when Dad was around, which was hardly ever. The rest of the time he and Amy had the house to themselves to do whatever they wanted. Apparently Amy always had boys over. They also had the added benefit of a large screen TV with ON DEMAND programming and a state-of-the-art computer among many other amenities. Evan also informed me that he'd always been able to drink with his friends at his father's house. He listed all of this as if it were completely normal behavior.

If I tried to voice my opinion on any of it I would get verbally trashed by Evan. Everything Dave has ever done has been projected onto me. I'm the one who "turned him against his father" his whole life. I'm the one who pushed my own kids away. It was so strange to hear Evan tell me the awful things that his father had done to him, yet continue to defend him if I suggested any of Dave's parenting was wrong. It was amazing to me how deep the brainwashing ran. No matter how horrific Dave's behavior, it always was and still is overlooked and even defended. No matter how loving and sacrificial my actions, I am always the bad parent.

Evan was living mostly with his father but he was still keeping in touch with me. This was not acceptable to Dave. He kicked Evan out of the house every time they had an argument. Evan would call me and tell me that he was "homeless again" and I would remind him, "Evan, you will never be homeless. You know you still have a bedroom here." He either pretended not to hear me or he changed the subject. Staying with me clearly was not an option.

One day in February of 2006, as I lay sick in bed with pneumonia, Evan called me and asked me to meet him at the courthouse. He said he'd been arrested and was being arraigned. My first thought was drugs or alcohol. Feeling my agitation he quickly told me, "Dad had me arrested for domestic abuse. I will explain when I see you. Please, come Mom."

I dragged my sick, clammy body down to the courthouse. An hour later Evan's case was continued and he came home with me. In the car on the way home Evan explained what had happened.

"Amy and I got into a verbal argument. Dad heard it from the other room. Without knowing what we were arguing about he stormed in and demanded that I get out of the house."

I felt my temperature rising and not just from the pneumonia as Evan relayed that he was happy to oblige his father but had told him that he wanted to collect some of his things from downstairs first. Dave had retorted that Evan couldn't get his things. They started arguing. Apparently Dave kicked Evan's feet out from under him and knocked him to the ground. Evan said that his father hovered over him then grabbed him by his collar.

"I got away from him and ran downstairs to get my stuff," Evan continued to explain. "I was running out the door when I heard Dad calling the police and telling them that I'd been causing a disturbance at the house. He said I'd refused to leave."

Evan had then driven straight to my house and called the police from my driveway. In my sickly stupor I hadn't realized he was out there.

"I told the cops that I was leaving when dad called them but they asked me to go back to Dad's house. When I got there the police arrested me."

I glanced at my son who was slumped in the seat beside me, biting his nails. I recognized the same mannerisms as when Evan would get verbally bashed by Dave as a child. He appeared to be in shock over what had just happened and, after a few minutes of silence, he continued to talk about it.

"The cops said that Amy had told them I'd pushed her. I never laid a hand on her, Mom!"

"Could you have inadvertently bumped into her?" I asked, trying to help him figure it all out.

"I didn't go anywhere near her. Our argument was verbal. Dad knows that!"

The next day, I went to the police station to see Nadine, the Domestic Violence Officer. She had come to know our family history all too well and had always been extremely sympathetic and supportive of me. She expressed to me her frustration at not being able to do more to help me.

"People like Dave have their phone calls sent upstairs," she explained, "to bypass the regular intake protocol. He has connections and he uses them frequently around here."

I could hear the helplessness in her voice. She told me that even the cops involved in this recent incident all felt that Evan had been "set up" by his father. They'd noted that when Amy was giving her testimony there was constant eye contact between her and Dave. They found that suspicious but they had no choice but to arrest Evan because of the corroborated stories between two witnesses.

Although I hated the circumstances behind it, I was so happy to have Evan home. I felt such relief as I watched him put his things away in his bedroom. I'd been so starved for my children that I could only thank God for his presence in my life and in my home. It was short lived.

On the second night that Evan spent with me he said that he'd told Elizabeth that he had slept in his car the night before. I looked at him incredulously as he explained that he didn't want Elizabeth, Amy, or his father to know he was staying with me.

"Evan, I find that very hurtful!"

"Sorry, Mom, I guess I just want them to feel bad for me."

Evan went to Elizabeth's for dinner and spent the night. I had stocked the fridge and cupboards with his favorite foods, bought him a DVD player for his bedroom and extended myself in every way I could think of to make him feel comfortable. He was in and out of my house during the day, but he would spend most nights at Elizabeth's house. It became clear to me that Elizabeth, Amy and Dave needed to believe that Evan wasn't with me at all. Even though my home was much more practical and convenient for Evan, as it was closer to his college, his work and the clinic, he chose to pacify his father.

Just a few days after the fiasco of his arrest, Evan joined Amy, Elizabeth, her husband, my little grandsons and Dave and his new girlfriend for a dinner to celebrate my grandson's last day of hockey. I listened in amazement as Evan told me all about it. It was as though none of the previous week's craziness had every happened.

"Dad's lawyer is going to defend me," Evan said, happily.

My head was screaming Stockholm Syndrome. Just like the prisoners of Stockholm, Evan had altered his experiences to accommodate Dave's reality. It was all so familiar; the abuse followed by the rescue. As I listened to Evan, I was reminded of my own pattern of justifying Dave's abuse.

"It's my fault, Mom," Evan lamented, "I just can't seem to get things right. Dad is such a good father."

I wanted to scream but there was nothing I could say.

Shortly after the big dinner with his father, Evan informed me that Amy was going to Colorado. The fact that I wasn't consulted about my high school daughter taking a week off from school to go to another state didn't surprise me but it hurt none the less. Amy told me that it was a spur of the moment decision. I realized that her father was paying for the trip but I was confused by the timing of it. No one would tell me why she was going away or who she was staying with. Coincidentally, Amy was in Colorado the same week that Evan was to return to court. The court domestic violence advocate called my home to explain that she couldn't get in touch with Amy. When she called me again, on the same morning that Evan was to appear in court, it hit me. The whole Machiavellian plan suddenly made sense.

Dave had arranged for Amy to be out of town rather than take a chance of her getting caught in his web of lies if they had to return to court. Amy's absence meant that the domestic violence case against Evan was dismissed.

Although refusing to disclose any particulars of her trip, Amy did ask me to watch her cat while she was in Colorado. She had gotten Mona as a kitten a year earlier and loved her like a baby. I didn't want her cat to be traumatized by being dropped off in a strange house and suggested Amy spend the night with me and Mona to help her adjust. That wasn't an option for Amy so I refused to cat-sit.

On the morning of her departure, Amy called to plead with me to take her kitty. "Please Mom, Dad said she can't stay here while I'm gone. Please take her!!!"

I suspected that Dave might get rid of Mona in Amy's absence so I reluctantly agreed to take her for the week. It took Mona three days to venture out of the closet and to finally trust me after I'd coaxed her with cat treats and calming pheromones that I'd bought at the pet store.

Amy returned from Colorado and asked me to keep Mona because Dave wouldn't allow the cat back into his house. He'd complained that Mona wasn't consistent about using the litter box and Amy defended her father's decision. "After all Mom, he just got the floors done!"

I knew that if I didn't keep Mona she would have to go to the shelter. I was amazed by how easily Amy had accepted Dave's decision about her precious cat. I still have Mona, twelve years later, and although she still has occasional litter box issues, I love her deeply and wouldn't give her up for anything.

Amy didn't come by to visit Mona once because Mona was in my world now. Nor did she call me or say goodbye before she left for college. My daughter emotionally detached from both of us and never looked back.

Evan did try living with me again. It lasted two weeks. Although I supported and respected him and stayed out of his business, it ended disastrously. It was extremely difficult to keep silent when Evan talked about his father and the unbelievable abuse he inflicted. I knew that to speak what I believed to be the truth was pointless and would only create conflict between us. All I ever wanted was a relationship with my children apart and aside from what is going on with their father. I asked Evan not to talk to me about his father or his father's lawyer, who was a hero in Dave's eyes. He seemed unable to do this and regaled me with stories I did not want to hear, almost as though he were goading me into an argument and daring me to dispute his truth.

One night I returned home from church only to be broadsided by Evan. I had worked all day and then traveled a half hour, each way, to visit my church. My spiritual tools were all I had to keep me going and I used them at every opportunity. I came home exhausted but spiritually refreshed. The last thing I wanted was a confrontation. As I walked in the door, Evan immediately started to try to goad me into a political debate.

After he'd criticized my political views he went on to parrot everything I'd heard from Dave for years. The axiom "Tell a lie enough times and it becomes the truth" kept passing through my mind as I listened to Evan blaming me for everything that had gone wrong in his life, including his drug addiction. He adamantly insisted that if I had used more discipline with him, and had let his father intervene more, then his addiction would never have happened. He also claimed that his alcohol problems were just "normal teen behavior" that I had overreacted to. He accused me of using him as a pawn just to get back at Dave. Apparently I'd moved to Western Mass. to take my children away from their father and I had relied my whole life on Dave's financial support. Evan yelled that his father paid for everything they did in addition to paying me child support. His ranting went on and on. It was as if the floodgates had opened and he couldn't stop himself. I pleaded with him to stop but he came up close and screamed in my face, "My father is a good man and a great parent!"

I was backed up against the wall, sobbing. "None of that is true. It's just the opposite of everything you said," I blurted, no longer in control of my own emotions. "Your father's a piece of shit!"

I regretted the words as soon as they left my mouth. I had been verbally and emotionally bashed for what seemed like an hour and I just couldn't take it anymore. I asked Evan to leave but he kept yelling at me. I ran outside and collapsed on the back deck.

When I could cry no more I gathered myself together enough to go back in the house. Evan was talking with Elizabeth on the phone. He was telling her how he couldn't stay with me because I insisted on trashing his father and had called him "a piece of shit." I knew that one slip would be used against me and told over and over and over.

I literally had to beg to see Amy on the night of her prom. She gave me five minutes to take a few pictures. I never got to hear about it or share the excitement with her like I had with Elizabeth after her prom. I had a chance to peek at her year book that Evan had brought to the house. She wrote her love to her father, her sister Elizabeth and Evan but not me.

Amy's high school graduation was one of the most painful days of my life. I knew what I was missing after my wonderful experience with Elizabeth's and Evan's graduation and I ached to share that joy with Amy. I knew her graduation would be difficult but I could not miss it. I asked my friend D to accompany me for emotional support. I don't know how I would have made it through without her.

Like all the other moms, I'd rushed to get up front after the kids threw their caps in the air. I hugged Amy tightly but felt her body stiffen. It was like hugging a board. She pulled away from me, looked at me and then politely said "Thank you for coming", as if she were talking to a neighbor who had decided to stop by. I thought back to my own high school graduation and couldn't imagine thanking my own mother for coming to it. Amy then turned to join her friends.

Shortly after Amy's graduation, Evan transferred to UMass in the western part of the state. He had weaned himself from the clinic and was doing well but I felt he wasn't ready for this big transition just yet. As usual, what I thought didn't matter. Dave made the decision for Evan to leave for college after encouraging him to take out student loans. I had no choice but to be supportive.

I'm not sure why Dave allowed it, but Evan asked me to take him to the university orientation. It was so exciting. In spite of my reservations I couldn't help but get caught up in thrill of seeing Evan go to college. I attended all the parent events, took notes, and went to lunch with Evan and the other parents in the cafeteria. I was in heaven for the day. It felt so good to be a parent again.

I made several trips out to the college, taking Evan to lunch and stores to pick up essentials. I sent him whatever money I could and prayed that he would have an awesome educational experience. At first he seemed to fall right into college life. He became active in political groups and told me he was enjoying his classes. Lurking in the background, however, was the pull of alcohol. Unable to resist, Evan partied too much and left the university after a year, laden with student loans for classes he didn't complete.

Evan came back to Oceanside and rented his own apartment. He started teaching music; something he had been doing in high school. Between teaching and performing gigs locally Evan was able to survive, but he said he always wanted to return to school. He took some classes at the community college and got involved in a singing group there. I attended his performances at the college. It was wonderful to see him in his element.

I've had very little communication with Elizabeth following our last court appearance. I'd mention to friends that when I did see my daughter I felt like the 'pod people' had taken her because while she looked like my Elizabeth, the child I had raised was not there. This woman was cold and aloof with me.

A few years after my first grandson was born, my second grandson arrived. I remember sitting in the hospital room with Elizabeth. Carl was also visiting with my first grandson. To say that I felt unwelcome is an understatement. I felt like the pariah in the room and wanted to jump out of my skin. I was full of emotion at seeing my beautiful daughter after just giving birth, and my two beautiful grandsons. But no one ever referred to me as 'grandma' or seemed pleased to even see me. As I watched the scene before me I flashed back to when Elizabeth had first dreamt about having children.

It had been at the beginning of my separation with Dave. Elizabeth and I were sitting at the dining room table when she looked at me lovingly and said, "Mom. I really want children but I don't want to stop working. I'm hoping that you will be able to watch your grandchildren while I'm at the bank. Knowing that my children are in your care is the only way that I would be able to keep working." It was so hard to reconcile that memory with the atmosphere in that hospital room. I kept my distance after that. I acknowledged birthdays with documentation of animals adopted on my grandchildren's behalf and donations I made in the name of Elizabeth. I don't know that these gestures were rebuffed but I do know that Evan chided me about a donation I gave in Elizabeth's name to the local Domestic Violence shelter. Evidently Elizabeth had told everyone and they had thought it was a joke. Evan scolded me, "Really Mom? What was your point? Did you think Elizabeth would appreciate that?"

I both anticipated and dreaded Amy's college graduation. My mother pride was swelling in me but I also knew that I would be putting myself through a lot of heartache. I called Amy and told her I needed a graduation ticket. There were only so many allotted per student and I couldn't risk being overlooked, which I knew was a real possibility.

Although I had driven up to the city where Amy attended college numerous times in the past four years, I always did so with trepidation. I never got used to all the one way streets and crazy drivers. The graduation was scheduled to begin at 11 am in a location not far from Amy's old dorm room. However, the parking situation is always a nightmare and I had a lot of angst about getting there on time. I called Elizabeth to ask her if we could ride up together. "I'm really nervous about the drive, parking and getting there on time. I also have to make sure I see Amy to get my ticket."

At first there was silence on the other end of the line. Finally Elizabeth responded, "Sorry Mom, I already have plans to go to the graduation, but good luck."

My heart sank. It was true that I didn't want to go alone, but I was also hoping that if Elizabeth and I went together it would give us a chance to bond a little.

I was fortunate enough to enlist the help of one of my dear friends, Tom, who has no problem driving in the city. On the Friday morning of the graduation ceremony we arrived in plenty of time to park then walked to the end of a long line of proud family members all celebrating their child's academic achievements. I called Amy's cell phone to get my ticket. She asked me where I was then assured me she'd get the ticket to me.

As Tom and I stood in line I noticed Dave walking toward me. He was holding my ticket tightly in his hand, close to his body. He stared at me as he taunted "Do you want your ticket?" I tried to take the ticket but he had a death grip on it. He finally released it, smirked, and then turned to reclaim his place in line up ahead of me where Elizabeth was waiting for him.

My friend Tom was incredulous. He shook his head and asked me if I wanted him to stick around until the line moved inside the building. I told him I would be fine. I don't think he believed me but he went off to stroll the city while I attended the gradation. Once again, it was Dave and Elizabeth in the forefront with me tagging along somewhere behind.

We finally filed into the auditorium and I saw Dave and Elizabeth make their way up to the front. The only seat I could find was towards the back. As with all of my children's milestones, I was overwhelmed. Amy's name was called and I stood up and cheered and cried with emotion.

After all the names were called out one of the speakers asked the graduates to look to their loved ones in the audience and give recognition to those who'd loved and supported them. Amy did not look in my direction. She beamed at Elizabeth in particular. Anyone watching would have thought that Dave and Elizabeth were Amy's parents. I was the ghost, again. I could hear myself cheering and I could feel the tears of pride wetting my cheeks but I felt invisible. I wanted to scream, "That's my daughter! That beautiful young woman getting her diploma. I gave birth to her. I raised her. I nurtured her. I am connected to her soul!" Instead, I swallowed my pain.

At the end of the long ceremony I stood at the back door waiting for Amy to walk through to congratulate her. The only people she acknowledged were Dave and Elizabeth. My friend Tom was waiting outside. We watched Elizabeth, Amy and Dave walk into another building. We overheard one of the graduates guiding guests into a reception. I hadn't been invited to the reception. I turned to Tom and said. "I need to get out of here."

I cried all the way home.

Tom was stunned. "I can't believe what I just saw." He already knew my story, but it didn't have as much impact until he saw it with his own eyes.

As painful as Amy's graduation was, I felt that school was my last link to her. I'd been able to call her and ask her what she needed and would take her shopping. I always felt she agreed out of necessity as she was struggling through school. However, she would be detached and distant. I stuffed my pain when I would look around her dorm room and see family pictures of everyone but me. When I took her out to eat I barely got any conversation from her. At one of our lunches she actually yelled at me for something I said about the salad I was eating and I started to cry. Unmoved, she could only say, "Let's go!" as she stood up and put her jacket on. It didn't stop me from going to visit her again. I would also send her care packages with food and rolls of quarters for laundry. I rarely got a response. Once she graduated, I didn't know how or when I would see her again.

Shortly after graduation I invited Amy to lunch. Surprisingly she agreed. As I was getting ready to leave my house to pick her up she called me. "Mom, I'm really tired. Could you just pick something up and we can eat here at my house?"

"Sure honey" I told her. I took her order and made my way to the house she was sharing with Evan and another roommate.

Amy was on the couch watching TV. She barely looked at me. I handed her the lunch I had bought her and she hardly touched it. I sat next to her in silence as she put her head back and fell asleep. I think she had the best of intentions but once she saw me in the flesh she detached in the only way she knew how. I ran my fingers through her hair and kissed her on the forehead before I left with tears in my eyes once again.

It became clear to me that trying to keep Amy in my life was only causing her more pain and internal conflict. I decided that I would only make minor gestures, and leave it up to her to pick up the ball if she chose to do so. So far she has not.

If there is a bright spot to this nightmare, it's that Paula and I eventually went ahead with the adoption we had talked about for so many years. Our reconnection during my fight for my children had brought us closer than ever. Paula's emails and phone calls during the most horrific months of my life were so supportive that I don't know how I would have gotten through it all without her. We had talked often, not only about the custody hearing but also about our similar pasts with our ex-husbands. We had both chosen controlling men who did not approve of our relationship. After waiting for over twenty years to make our bond official, we walked arm-in-arm into the same court room that had severed me from my biological children and within five minutes, Paula became my daughter.

Donna Buiso

Chapter 19

BATTERED MOTHER'S TESTIMONY PROJECT REFLECTION

It was in May, 2002, when women who'd experienced similar stories of abuse from their mates and from the probate court system had been interviewed from all over the state for the Battered Mother's Testimony Project (BMTP). Over two hundred stories had been gathered. I could never have imagined that it would have so little impact. A few changes were made. Senator Cheryl Jacques of Massachusetts wrote a human rights report. It caused a little bit of a stir and a few minor changes in the law, but then it was forgotten. We are forgotten.

Years later, our pain as mothers is still not being taken seriously or validated. My greater concern is with the children who are growing up, or have grown up, in this environment. People who don't understand this usually try to placate us by saying that 'when the kids get older they'll change or understand.' For many children it is Stockholm Syndrome. The brainwashing runs too deep. It is the same at twelve, nineteen, or twenty-six. What is the long-term effect of cutting your mother out of your life or having her cut out of your life when you don't have any say? What is the long-term effect of growing up with a narcissistic sociopath? The court doesn't care. Probate Court is supposed to be about children and families. The truth is that Probate Court couldn't care less about my children. I believe my involvement with the BMTP actually hindered my case because I had mentioned Judge Hatcher in my testimony.

The real power lies with the judges who decide these cases. I believe the judges who decided my future (or lack thereof) with my children cannot possibly, nor care to understand the destruction their decisions triggered. They devastated not one but four lives, not to mention the grandparents and extended family members involved. As Judge Hatcher admits, in a follow-up email to the reporter who wrote the article that prompted me to share my story, "Once a decision is made," he says he "rarely mulls it over again."

EXHIBIT W: Quote from Judge Hatchet

A judge has to weigh information coming from all those involved in the case to determine "the best interest of the child," _____ said.

"There are cases that you don't know for sure what happened, obviously, and you don't know if it's the right decision, but you believe you made the right decision," _____ said about deciding custody issues. "I've looked at cases and agonized over making the decision one way or the other and finally said, 'I've got to do this.'"

Once a decision is made, however, he rarely mulls it over again, _____ wrote in an email following his interview with the Times.

I've had to live with his decisions and will probably never get the opportunity to recoup the bond I had once shared with my children. Although I have tried to never give up on my children I feel like I always hit a wall. The sadness of this loss lives in my heart like a cancer that can't be cured. I'm left with nothing but my voice and my memories. There are so many memories I should have but never had the opportunity to make with my children. Not only did I miss major milestones but also Christmas, Thanksgiving and Easter almost every year for more than fifteen years. I have also lost tender years with my grandchildren and they have lost their time with me.

Over the years, Elizabeth has made some efforts to include me in holiday dinners but I've always felt tolerated more than welcomed. Elizabeth and Amy would chat in a corner while Carl and my cousin Gina ignored me completely.

Watching Elizabeth 'mothering' Amy was excruciating. Conversations always seemed to become about Dave and whatever plans my children might have with him. I listened to the conversations that involved a world that I didn't live in anymore. I'd sit alone and wonder what I was doing there. I may have been in the same room as my children but I was still invisible. No one cared what I had to say. I'd leave feeling sick and disoriented, suspecting that Elizabeth's invitation was more about obligation than love.

As much as I always want to be around my children, I have the burning need to feel connected. Sitting with them and feeling a million miles away is as hard as not being with them at all. I long for the days when we freely hugged, laughed and bonded over all we loved, from music to our love for each other. I long for the days when we trusted each other and had no need to feel guarded.

There was a time when Elizabeth used to buy me the most meaningful cards, expressing her undying love for me. For one birthday, decades ago, she gave me a framed photograph of dancing dolphins which still hangs on the wall in my bedroom. She knew how much I loved dolphins and always put love and care into choosing her gifts for me. We have, on sporadic occasions, tried to reconnect, but whenever we come close there is usually an incident involving Dave or his family that stops our progress in its tracks.

I can't remember a time, in the last fifteen years, when Amy has put her arms around me, told me she loves me, or has given me a meaningful card. I heard from my Evan that she lives within ten minutes of my home. If I get a birthday or Christmas gift to her through Evan I may or may not get a text message saying 'thank you'.

Several years ago, Evan did give me a Mother's Day card that made me sob. He expressed such love and credited me with being a "loving mother" and his "biggest supporter." While I cherish this card, it also reminds me of how much I miss that show of love.

When it comes to my children I am always wrong. There is no amount of good that I can do to change that. It seems that there is also no amount of bad that Dave can do to shake their image of him. I believe the Probate Court's treatment of us reinforced our children's perception of their father having all the power.

Dave had blatantly ignored court orders, he'd lied and assassinated my character, and although he had restraining orders against him and DSS found him neglectful, the court never once even reprimanded him. Instead, it fully enforced his ability to 'erase' me from my children's lives.

Where's the justice in that?

We have built a society based on this dysfunctional system. Power and money are the bottom line. Justice has become a business at the expense of human beings. This is an epidemic that cannot be ignored. Hopefully some of these children will break free of their mental and emotional constraints, but too many of them will grow up to continue the legacy of abuse.

This abuse of people and power must be recognized and confronted.

Chapter 20

EPIDEMIC

As I said at the beginning of this memoir, this is not just my story. I want to acknowledge the voices of the women I met as I fought in the courts for my children. Their stories may contain different details to mine, but they all share the same theme: our abusive ex-husbands set out to destroy us after we left them.

In each case, there is manipulation of children who have been emotionally starved of their father's love and attention. When this is suddenly offered to them they are conflicted and want to satisfy what they have craved for their whole lives. The price is to abandon their mothers. This process is done so subtly and covertly that the children don't even realize that it's happening. They may even come up with reasons that have been planted by their father. These mothers have been labeled 'emotionally unstable', 'crazy', or 'weak'. In my case, there was absolutely no documentation of any mental unbalance of any kind, yet Dave used it against me over and over until others started to repeat it. The labels are usually vague and without fact, or, in the cases of the cleverest of manipulators, there will be a grain of truth to build on, as with Evan and the knife. As I discovered, the lies get told so much that they become a new truth. It is a clever but subtle form of brainwashing. By allowing and enabling this kind of behavior, the court causes destruction of lives and families instead of carrying out the purpose of protecting lives and families. Years of hearing of probate horror stories culminated with the one that spurred me to finally tell my story.

In 2012, the local newspaper ran a report on why probate judges are not accountable for their decisions. This report was in reference to the story I mentioned at the beginning of this memoir about a mother's fight to protect her child. The reporter had been following this case closely since 2009 and wrote that the mother's complaint was directed at Judge Hatchet, The article states, "A pair of complaints against a local judge likely won't ever see the light of day, as the board that probes judiciary conduct deliberates in secrecy."

After reading this, I contacted the mother, C, who expressed to me her frustration and disbelief that her ex-husband was not in jail for his crimes against their son. I was sitting in court when the judge, unmoved by compelling testimony from a police officer, the child's teacher and other testimony, begrudgingly stated that visitation with the father was suspended "for now" because he "had no choice based on the DNA evidence" against him. This evidence was semen found on the child's pajamas that belonged to his father and a second unidentified individual.

C In Her Own Words

I'm a mother who has been fighting for years in probate court to protect my son. He was being sexually abused, raped and tortured by his own father and someone else in his father's company. I am still fighting because the court is not one hundred percent convinced of the abuse.

The abuse started with me in February, 2006, after I moved to the U.S from Brazil. From February through April of that year my child's father tried to kill me twice. I was initially too afraid to report this. Then one night he showed me his "private" internet site of photographs of people, including a child, being sexually tortured and he warned me that this is what would happen to me if I "talked too much." I immediately reported what I'd seen to the local police. A forensic examiner confiscated, then searched his computer and reported that twenty-four images of women "being sexually tortured" were found. My child's father was arrested but was released after ten days because I was too scared to testify after my husband told me the D.A. was his friend.

During our divorce, the judge wanted me to agree to shared custody with my child's father, despite all this evidence against him. I didn't speak or understand English well at the time and was totally ignored when I claimed that I believed my husband was sexually abusing my son. I tried hard to explain myself many times in court but I was never heard. I felt pressured to sign the divorce papers which were never read to me. I didn't understand what I was signing. I would never have agreed to visitation between my son and his abusive father.

At the beginning, I thought just a few people went through this kind of horrific ordeal, but I have now met many mothers who have had their children taken from them, as if they were the criminals. What is even more sickening is that the court system knows the children's pain and their vulnerability and that they are unable to protect themselves from these monsters.

Throughout my whole process I heard from agencies and in court that my son was "too young to be believed" and that I was a "pitiable" and "over-protective mother." This makes me sick and God knows that I wish they were right. I do wish I was crazy. At least then I would know that it was all just in my imagination. However, the abuse has happened to my son so many times that he says he wishes that he had never been born.

It was only after irrefutable DNA evidence that his father's "sperm and semen fluid" was found on my son's pajamas that the judge temporarily suspended my son's visits with his father. The judge concluded in his report, however, that he believes it's in the best interest of the child that in the future, father and son "can restore their healthy relationship."

Today, my son lives in imminent fear of any future contact with his father. I try to explain to him that bad things happen but that good things do too, and a lot will depend on the choices that he makes in life. The fact is, I fought as hard as I could for so long but could not protect my son. The years of torture at the hands of his father have left him with permanent scars that no one, not even the best surgeon in the world, can remove because they are internal and psychological.

The whole system appears to work really hard, but not to protect innocent children like my son. We mothers fight with our hearts and will give our money and time for the safety of our children while the court works against us. I used to believe in the law. I'd always heard that in America the law works. The people I met who were fighting to protect their children were all obeying the law but their rights to protect their children were violated. I no longer believe in the justice system. I respect the law because I have to but I do not believe in it. I do believe in God's justice. That is, above all, something we can accept or not. It is something that I choose to accept and not because I have to.

M Pedophile Father Gets Custody Of His Kids

M found me through the Battered Mother's Testimony Project. She had an inheritance from her deceased parents. It wasn't long into her marriage before she realized that her husband, T, was squandering their money and had incurred a huge financial debt. He also cheated on her and became abusive to her physically and emotionally. They separated shortly after the birth of their second daughter.

T would not pay child support. M appeared in probate court in Oceanside before Judge Fake to explain the financial bind she was in. Judge Fake did not give T any consequences for non-payment of child support but he did tell M to borrow money from her family.

T suddenly started to pay child support after he remarried. He also secretly campaigned to get custody of the girls, slowly and deliberately brainwashing them against their mother. The court awarded T custody of the girls, solely on their request, and revoked the child support. M lost her children and the new home she had just bought for the three of them.

Several months later, T made the newspapers because he was being sued in a sexual harassment case. M read his court files and discovered that her ex had exposed himself at work and police had uncovered hundreds of child porn sites on his computer, both at work and at home. M's first thought was for her children. The scandal caused T to make plans to move with his new wife and M's girls to another state. Frantic, M filed motions in court to regain custody of her children.

Everything she filed for was denied. Judge Terrible even denied counseling for herself and her children. He appeared unfazed by the charges against T and referred to him by his first name when he assured him that he'd try to wrap up the court proceedings within three weeks so as to help expedite his move. This was the same judge who'd made me wait for months and then derailed my trial. The GAL was Ms. Pustule, who was also involved in my case, and she recommended no visitation for M.

M packed up her car and moved to the state her children were now living in. It was a risk that didn't work out. She couldn't find a job that paid enough to survive and she ended up living in her car.

B Psychologist Refuses To Get His Suicidal Son Therapy

B was standing outside the courthouse crying when I first met her. When I asked if she was okay she started ranting about the unfairness of the court and said she was scared to death about what was happening to her life. I could only sympathize.

B had three children and had been in an abusive marriage for thirty years. Her ex-husband was a mean drunk who told her that no matter how much he drank, she was still ugly. Her middle child had problems with depression and had talked about suicide. B feared for his life but her husband, a psychologist, refused to acknowledge that their child needed help. He was what I call a "sophisticated batterer", who, like Dave, was extremely conscious of his image. He wouldn't allow counseling for his son because of what others may think about it.

A couple of years prior to our meeting, B explained that she'd woken up one morning to find her son dead from hanging himself. This jolted her enough to leave the marriage. Her ex immediately went on a campaign to financially annihilate her. She looked to the court for help. B said she'd felt shocked and disoriented when she was pressured into signing agreements that she would never have made in a rational state of mind. As B was leaving the court she heard her ex and his lawyer laughing at the financial burdens they were able to stick her with.

Judge Terrible had ordered B to sell her beautiful home where she had lived for thirty years. Although she had a Master's Degree, she hadn't worked outside of the home for thirty years because she 'wasn't allowed'. She had raised three children and helped her husband build his career. B had showed the court documentation from her therapist outlining how she suffers from posttraumatic stress disorder and wasn't able to focus enough to hold down a job for long. This didn't prevent Judge Terrible from barking at her to "Get a job!"

B's youngest child moved in with her father after he lavished her with gifts and attention. She soon cut B out of her life. B said she lost two children; one through death and one through parental alienation. She often says that she should have stayed in her abusive marriage to avoid the heartache that followed her leaving.

U Judge Retaliates For Media Coverage And Misplaced Support Of Pedophile Father

U told me that she started having problems with her little boy when he was three. She had already divorced the child's father but he still had visitation. The little boy said and did things that showed signs of severe sexual abuse, like soiling himself. Through counseling it came out that the abuser was the child's father. To U's relief, her ex would often disappear only to resurface months later. During his absence the child's symptoms subsided and his emotional health seemed to improve.

Eventually the child's father decided he wanted to start seeing his boy again and U refused. Her ex brought his appeal for visitation to Oceanside Probate. Documentation from the counseling sessions was presented to Judge Terrible, and, although no one denied the allegations, Judge Terrible still sided with the boy's father and agreed that he had a right to visitation with his son, in spite of all the expert's recommendations against it.

U, out of desperation, called the media. After the local newspaper published a story about her situation, Judge Terrible retaliated by accusing her of being more concerned with publicity than with her child. He ordered her to pay restitution to her ex for his travel expenses incurred to visit with his son. The judge also ordered U to do community service on what she referred to as the 'chain gang'. She was the only person we've ever heard of from Probate Court to be loaded into a van with criminals to pick up trash on the side of the road.

After being absent again for about a year, U's ex suddenly filed a contempt against U for not letting him have visitation. U requested a different judge or a change in venue. Her attorney explained that Judge Terrible would not give up this case because she had filed a complaint with the Judicial Committee against him. I was in court with U that day. Judge Terrible had a female police officer ready to take U to Framingham State Women's Prison if she didn't turn her son over for visitation. We both knew that if she was locked up her ex might get full custody. U had to let her boy go to the man who sexually abused him. She told me that she prays for the times that her ex becomes bored and disappears again.

N Control Using Real Estate

I had known N for over thirty years. We'd met as single mothers to our oldest daughters. We went our separate ways when N moved in with C and I married Dave. Like me, she had two more children.

C was an alcoholic and abusive. N tolerated the abuse as she continued to hold a job and take care of her children. After twenty-five years of living together, C came home and told N that he'd fallen in love with someone twenty years younger. He was surprised when N asked him to leave. After he took off with his younger woman he showed little interest in their teenage children. The youngest daughter became deeply troubled and got caught up in drugs and alcohol.

N came back into my life a few years later when she heard what I was going through with my children. She had been through it and wanted to help me. Her children had grown up and left home but she was still living in the house that she and C co-owned. The need for repairs on the house accumulated to the point of holes in the walls and floors and deteriorated plumbing but she could get no help from C. When she could no longer afford the upkeep N tried to sell the house for the value of the land.

A buyer agreed to buy the house for the land but C refused to sell his half. It was his last means of control. N took C to Oceanside Probate Court three times. She took pictures of the deplorable conditions she was living in but Judge Terrible just shook his head. C told the judge that he wanted time to buy N out. Judge Terrible gave him a couple of months to come up with the money. At the end of the agreed time C still hadn't raised the funds so Judge Terrible gave him more time. This is the same judge who had told B to sell her home to the next buyer. In the meantime, N was spending thousands of dollars on lawyer fees until she exhausted herself financially.

N gave up going back to court and rented a room because her house no longer had heat. In the summertime she returned to her house even though it didn't have hot water.

C had had nothing to do with their daughter for years, but when he found out that she was in a psychiatric unit out of state he saw his opportunity to grasp more control. C convinced their daughter that N was the source of all her problems. N has not seen her daughter since. She has been completely cut her out of her life.

L Jail? Really?

L is another woman who found me through my work with the BMTP. She called me and told me her story a few years ago.

L is a professional whose ex-husband got custody of her two young sons even though he is an abuser. He managed to convince the court that L was mentally unstable although she works in the field of mental health. She had all of her rights stripped from her where her children are concerned. They, like a lot of children in these environments, are now afraid to show or feel love for her.

After L managed to get the court to agree to counseling for her and her children she started to make progress with her oldest son. During one of their visitations her son said that his father was abusive to him and that he didn't want to go back to him. The boy, at fourteen, was at an age where the court is supposed to listen to his wishes. L called her ex to tell him that their son wanted to stay with her. The father responded by calling the police, having L arrested for kidnapping, and then having a restraining order imposed upon her. Her son was returned to his father.

A few weeks later, L's ex was abusing her oldest boy. The boy grabbed a knife and tried to hurt his father. The police took the boy away and put him in a psychiatric facility. There were no charges filed against the father. L is afraid her child will try to kill himself because he has alluded to it many times. She would tell me, "All I want to do is to parent my children."

L ended up in Framingham State Women's Prison for violating her restraining order by trying to contact her children. There was no trail, no jury and no bail. She was strip searched and locked up with murderers and thieves for over a month.

Q From Riches To Rags

I met Q when I started at a new job. She had worked as a flight attendant for twenty years and then as an RN. I felt an instant connection to her and could sense that she was carrying around a lot of pain that she didn't talk about. I finally heard parts of her story. She had a son she hadn't seen or heard from in five years. He was her only biological child. The last time she had seen him was when he'd graduated from high school.

I had learned that Q was homeless and living in her car when she came to work at the restaurant. She explained that she'd been married to a wealthy CEO who was a physical and emotional abuser. Upon their separation, he had viciously fought her on the finances until she agreed to let it all go. All she wanted was her son and child support for him through college. She said that her ex had little to do with the boy and that he agreed to her terms. However, as their son got closer to graduating, Q's ex made his move. By the time her son graduated, Q had been shoved out of his life and the courts refused to help her.

Q's ex, like mine, had worked on her family. Q is also estranged from her own mother who had allied with her ex.

E Can't Call Me 'Mom'

E's story is different only from the financial aspect. She has been able to maintain some financial security, at least for the time being. The rest of the story is the same.

When her older daughter was a teen and her youngest close to it, their father began to cheat on E. She said the fights were bad enough to force her to escape to her mom's home in Oceanside. It was supposed to be temporary but E's ex quickly moved his girlfriend into their home, forcing E to stay in Oceanside. The courts did nothing to help her.

E and her husband were supposed to have shared custody of their daughters but their father used his time with them to poison his daughters against their mother. E told me that her ex insisted that her children call her E instead of Mom. The two girls have been through hell. One suffers from depression and the other from drugs and alcohol. E has been pushed out of their lives.

Although E advocated for counseling and help for her youngest daughter, her ex continually refused to include E in a plan to help their daughter. Everyone in 'the system' also ignored her rights as a mother even though she has documentation proving she had 'shared' custody.

At one point, E's ex was pushing his youngest daughter and she struck back at him. He called the police. After this incident the girl decided to move in with her mother. She had been so damaged that she verbally and physically assaulted E. No matter how much E tried to show her daughter love and affection the girl rebuffed her. In spite of the abuse, she returned to her father's house and continued to abuse drugs.

Although not perfect, every one of these women are intelligent, educated and kind hearted. None of us had been institutionalized or had felonies or crimes on record before our efforts to protect our children in the courts. None of us deserved to end up penniless and childless. I have only touched the tip of the iceberg on each of these women. Each one could write a book about their stories.

There are also many other mothers whom I met since the BMTP. There was the woman who called me a few years ago to tell me of her experience in Oceanside Probate Court with Judge Hatcher. She also was married to an abuser and the judge let him take everything. She fought to keep her house for her two boys who were in their last years of high school, but the judge made her move and told her the boys were old enough to "adjust."

I worked with a woman whose husband said he was going to kill her before morning. Oceanside Court gave him custody of their three children because "she abandoned them." The father then refused to let her near her children.

Although the overwhelming majority of 'victims' of the court were mothers, I did know of a father whose wife got into drugs and left him to raise their preteen children. The children did not want to have visitation with their mother because her time spent with them involved nothing but drug runs. In this instance, Judge Terrible sided with the mother and insisted on their visitation. The man's son resorted to stealing his mother's drugs to bring to his father so he could show the judge. This is what it took for Judge Terrible to finally suspend the mother's visitation.

I could go on and on but it would take another full book. We mothers have appealed to the Federal Government, Amnesty International, The National Organization for Women, The AFL-CIO, the ACLU, domestic violence groups and many others, to no avail. No one takes seriously what we and our children have been through.

It reminds me of the days when a rape victim was questioned about what she might have done to get raped. Yes, we married abusers. Maybe we should have been smarter. Maybe we should have left sooner. This shouldn't mean that we suffer for the remainder of our days as well as our children and other family members. My parents, by not being allied with Dave, were alienated by their grandchildren. My Dad died at eighty-two with a broken heart, especially over Elizabeth. He was forty-five when she was born and she had been the light of his life. There seems to be a mindset that in a 'domestic' relationship the abuser has different rights than if the abuser were a boss, a neighbor or a co-worker.

In my case, and in each of the cases I've mentioned above, the abuser walks through life causing destruction and chaos to everyone in his path. Yet he is the only one who remains unfazed and unscathed. The system and the people in it have enabled him. We mothers call Probate Court the 'House of Evil'. For each and every one of us it couldn't be named more appropriately. It is a place where the facts don't matter and not everyone gets a voice. It's a place to be unjustifiably character assassinated and stripped of parental and human rights. It is a place where we lost our children to the devil and can no longer protect them.

Had my ex-husband used a physical weapon against me I believe the court may have protected me, but I will never recover from the losses that I have suffered over my children and grandchildren. I pray that someday they will have memories return to them of me as a loving mother and maybe give me some credit for the loving people they have become. As my grandchildren grow older I hope they will take the initiative to get to know me and realize that I have always loved them, even though it was from afar.

Throughout it all, I have gained strength I could never have imagined. I will never again allow someone to abuse me, not even those I love the most. I know that I have flaws, but a lack of profound loving and caring for my children is not one of them. I did the best I could and know without a doubt that I did not deserve what I got: not from my ex-husband, not from the courts and not even from my now grown children.

I spent so many years in courts and so much money on useless lawyers that I am spent. I used to tell the actors in probate, "I could just walk away, live my own life and pursue my dreams. Why would I put myself through this? I keep fighting because of my love for my children."

I'm tired but I do what I need to do to survive. My voice is my strength. It's all I have left. I will continue to use it, not just for myself, but for the children and for all the mothers who find themselves fighting to protect their family in court. I have been left with nothing but my voice and I will not die without being heard.

ABOUT THE AUTHOR

Donna Buiso lives on Cape Cod, Massachusetts. In 2002, she shared her story of how she lost her children when she testified at the Massachusetts State House Grand Staircase for the Battered Mothers Testimony Project (BMTP). In the many years since then, she has heard from countless mothers with similar stories. She hopes that this memoir might help them to also have a voice.

Donna Buiso

Starry Night Publishing

Everyone has a story...

Don't spend your life trying to get published! Don't tolerate rejection! Don't do all the work and allow the publishing companies reap the rewards!

Millions of independent authors like you, are making money, publishing their stories now. Our technological know-how will take the headaches out of getting published. Let "Starry Night Publishing.Com" take care of the hard parts, so you can focus on writing. You simply send us your Word Document and we do the rest. It really is that simple!

The big companies want to publish only "celebrity authors," not the average book-writer. It's almost impossible for first-time authors to get published today. This has led many authors to go the self-publishing route. Until recently, this was considered "vanity-publishing." You spent large sums of your money, to get twenty copies of your book, to give to relatives at Christmas, just so you could see your name on the cover. Now, however, the self-publishing industry allows authors to get published in a timely fashion, retain the rights to your work, keeping up to ninety-percent of your royalties, instead of the traditional five-percent.

We've opened up the gates, allowing you inside the world of publishing. While others charge you as much as fifteen-thousand dollars for a publishing package, we charge less than five-hundred dollars to cover copyright, ISBN, and distribution costs. Do you really want to spend all your time formatting, converting, designing a cover, and then promoting your book, because no one else will?

Our editors are professionals, able to create a top-notch book that you will be proud of. Becoming a published author is supposed to be fun, not a hassle.

At Starry Night Publishing, you submit your work, we create a professional-looking cover, a table of contents, compile your text and images into the appropriate format, convert your files for eReaders, take care of copyright information, assign an ISBN, allow you to keep one-hundred-percent of your rights, distribute your story worldwide on Amazon, Barnes & Noble and many other retailers, and write you a check for your royalties. There are no other hidden fees involved! You don't pay extra for a cover, or to keep your book in print. We promise! Everything is included! You even get a free copy of your book and unlimited half-price copies.

In four short years, we've published more than fifteen-hundred books, compared to the major publishing houses which only add an average of six new titles per year. We will publish your fiction, or non-fiction books about anything, and look forward to reading your stories and sharing them with the world.

We sincerely hope that you will join the growing Starry Night Publishing family, become a published author and gain the world-wide exposure that you deserve. You deserve to succeed. Success comes to those who make opportunities happen, not those who wait for opportunities to happen. You just have to try. Thanks for joining us on our journey.

www.starrynightpublishing.com

www.facebook.com/starrynightpublishing/

61816591R00126

Made in the USA
Charleston, SC
27 September 2016